MARKETING MANAGEMENT

JAYSHREE PARMAR

CONTENTS

Lecture No.		Page Nos.
1	Introduction to Marketing	1 - 8
2	The Marketing Environment	9 - 16
3	Strategic Planning	17 - 24
4	Marketing Planning	25 - 32
5	Marketing Research	33 - 39
6	Consumer Buying Behaviour	40 - 49
7	Business Buyer Behaviour	50 - 53
8	Segmentation, Targeting and Positioning	54 - 60
9	Products & Services	61 - 67
10	Product Strategies	68 - 75
11	Branding & Packaging	76 - 85
12	Pricing	86 - 94
13	Distribution	95 - 102
14	Promotion	103 - 109
15	Advertising	110 - 116
16	Sales Promotion & Public Relations	117 - 121
17	Personal Selling & Sales Management	122 - 129
18	Customer Satisfaction & Care	130 - 138
19	Managing Marketing	139 - 151

MARKETING MANAGEMENT

> TOPIC: INTRODUCTION TO MARKETING
> LECTURE: *1*

WHAT IS MARKETING?

Marketing activities are designed to satisfy consumers and meet organisational needs. In a commercial business, this specifically means generating revenue and contributing to profitability.

Marketing has its origins in simple barter. Today, it is a highly sophisticated series of activities designed to fill gaps in the marketplace and add value to exchanges with consumers. The foundation concepts of marketing are exchange, products, sellers, buyers and satisfaction.

It is important to study marketing because it is pervasive in our daily lives and has powerful effects on individual consumers, businesses and society. Marketing is very important to business profitability and it plays a role of growing significance in establishing competitiveness domestically and internationally.

Marketing has evolved dramatically since the earliest days of simple barter. It continues to evolve as society changes. Initially, marketing was an individual activity. Because of the Industrial Revolution, it became oriented toward organisational activities. Dominant business operating philosophies have evolved from production, product and selling orientations, to the marketing concept philosophy. Some marketers now practice societal marketing where the good of society is a primary consideration in how the business operates.

Marketers use McCarthy's original concept of the **4 Ps**: **Product, Price, Place** and **Promotion** to satisfy consumers and achieve organisational goals. Later additions to the marketing mix variables increasing them to **7 Ps** are: **Politics, Pride** and **People**. Also, for services 7 Ps are suggested: **Physical Evidence, Processes** and **People** (the 'soft' elements of the Marketing Mix as opposed to original 4 Ps which are the 'hard' elements of the marketing mix.).
These are the tools marketers use to add value to exchanges with consumers and achieve their strategic goals.

Definitions of marketing
Various definitions of Marketing exist:
- Marketing is the managerial function involved with identifying, anticipating and satisfying customer needs profitably. *(CIM - UK)*
- Marketing is a social and managerial process by which individuals and groups obtain what they need and want through creating and exchanging products and value with others. *(P.Kotler)*
- All the activities inside and outside the organisation which aim at the satisfaction and excitement/enthusiasm of the customer profitably. *(Theo Hadjiyannis - CIM)*

Understanding the Critical Role of Marketing in Organisations and Society
Marketing is part of all of our lives and touches us in some way every day. Most people have been involved with marketing from an early age and know more about marketing than they think. The marketing system has given us a standard of living that our ancestors could not have imagined. Many large and small companies make up this marketing system. Marketing is a key factor in business success

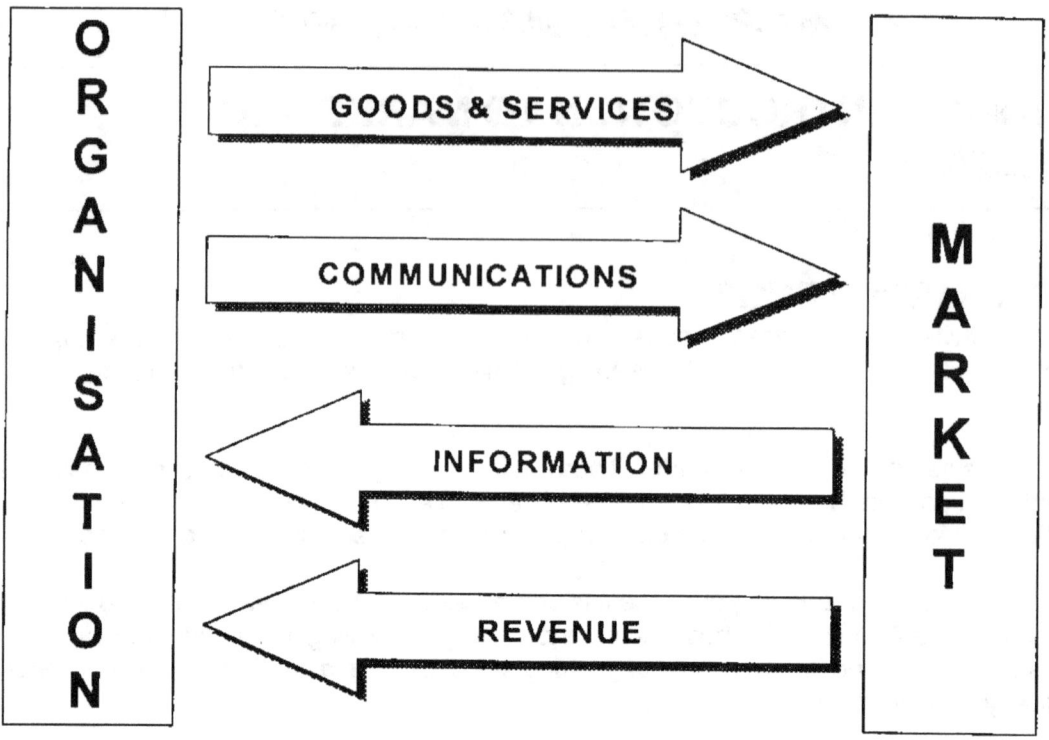

All organisations use marketing:
- **Corporations**
- **Government**: The Ministry of Health promoting the National Health Plan
- **Political Parties**: Promoting their politicians during elections
- **Hospitals**: An American hospital, competing for maternity patients, offered a steak and champagne dinner (Sales Promotion) with candlelight for new parents. Other hospitals, in an effort to attract physicians have installed services such as saunas, chauffeurs and private tennis courts
- **Schools**: University of Dundee MBA program (Distribution)
- **Churches**: Many churches are redesigning their service offering to better meet the needs of their target audience so as to keep members and financial support e.g. Second Mass on Sundays at 10.00 am
- **National Guard**: A marketing plan to attract Non-Commission Officers for a 5-year period
- **Postal Service**: Launch of new and collection stamps

Marketing for **Profit** and **Non-Profit** organisations differs in terms of relative emphasis on objectives:
- Company profit
- Consumer want satisfaction
- Public interest

Satisfying customer needs (creating utility) through the exchange process
Needs are satisfied through the Creation of a Marketing Mix (4Ps):
- **P**roduct is the offer made in the marketplace
- **P**rice is the amount charged for the product
- **P**lace (Distribution) is where, when and how the product is made available to the market to satisfy Target Market(s) (customers)
- **P**romotion is how marketers communicate with consumers and includes:

- Advertising
- Personal Selling
- Sales Promotions & Merchandising
- Public Relations
- Direct Marketing

- **What is selling?** Selling is exchanging what is made for what is desired
- **What is promotion?** Promotion is making known what is offered
- **What is merchandising?** Merchandising is the display of products

NEEDS, WANTS and DEMANDS
What are needs?
1. **Needs** - emerge from a state of felt deprivation. Needs are the perception of the opportunity to enhance or protect one's self and self-image
2. **Wants** - the form taken by human needs as they are shaped by culture and individual experience
3. **Demands** - are wants backed by buying power.

Need Satisfaction in a marketing exchange means that a gap has been filled for the buyer, a tension is reduced when a need or want is satisfied

Consumer Satisfaction - is very important to marketers and consumers, but it is not always clear what it takes to satisfy consumers and satisfaction is often a function of situations and circumstances.

WHAT ARE PRODUCTS?
Products are anything offered for sale, rent or use to satisfy a need or want, the things of value that are the offers marketers make to consumers. Products are need satisfiers.

ORIGINS OF MARKETING.
When did marketing first evolve?
- Division of labour.
- Specialisation.
- Exchange of goods, Barter etc.

Exchange is key to marketing, without an exchange there is no need to market.

EXCHANGE AND UTILITY
Exchange is the act of obtaining a desired object from someone by offering something in return. Exchange is only one of many ways to obtain a desired object. Exchange is the core concept of marketing.

Conditions of exchange include:
- At least two parties must participate.
- Each party has something that might be of value to the other party
- Each party believes it is appropriate or desirable to deal with the other party
- Each party must be free to accept or reject the other's offer.
- Each party is capable of communication and delivery

The exchange process creates **Utility**.

Utility is the satisfaction, value or usefulness a user receives from a good or a service. When you purchase a car, you give up less (in £s) than the value of the car (to you) ...the ability to get you from A to B, safely, in a timely manner etc.

There are four types of utility:
1. **Form**: production of the good, driven by the marketing function e.g. REGIS turns cream, sugar and milk into ice-cream.
2. **Place**: making the product available where customers will buy the product e.g. Ice-cream van at a construction site, beach, supermarket, kiosk etc.
3. **Time**: make product available when customers want to buy the product
4. **Possession**: once you own the product, do what you want with it, i.e. eat it, offer it

An example of a service that offers all types of utility: a 24-hour ice-cream delivery service.

Marketing performs the exchange functions that make the total utility of the product a reality to consumers.

Transactions - are a trade between two parties that involves at least two things of value agreed-upon conditions, a time of agreement and a place of agreement.

Sellers - the exchange partners that make the offer to buyers.

Buyers - individuals, households, businesses, professionals and others who are party to marketing exchanges and seek to satisfy their needs and wants from the exchange.

Relationships - are long-term commitments smart marketers build with valued customers.

Markets - consist of the set of actual and potential buyers of a product. A market consists of all the potential customers sharing a particular need or want who might be willing and able to engage in exchange to satisfy that need or want

Marketing -means working with markets to bring about exchanges for the purpose of satisfying human needs and wants.

THE MARKETING MANAGEMENT PHILOSOPHIES

Marketing Management is defined as the analysis, planning implementation and control of programs designed to create, build and maintain beneficial exchanges with target buyers for the purpose of achieving organisational objectives.

- It can be simply described as carrying out the tasks that achieve desired exchanges, between the corporation and its customers.

- Marketing efforts should be guided by a marketing philosophy. Decisions about the weight given to the interests of the organisation, customers and society need to be made by marketing managers.

There are five alternative concepts under which organisations conduct their marketing activities:

1. THE PRODUCTION CONCEPT
The production concept is the philosophy that consumers will favour products that are available and highly affordable and that management should therefore focus on improving production and distribution efficiency.

The production concept is useful when:
- Demand for a product exceeds the supply to increase profit, the organisation focuses on production efficiencies knowing all output can be sold.
- The product's cost is too high and improved productivity is needed to bring it down.

A typical quote during the production era: *"Doesn't matter whet colour car you want, as long as it is black."* Henry Ford about his Model T Ford car

Dominant era: From mid C19th to early C20th, industrial revolution etc.

2. THE PRODUCT CONCEPT
The product concept is the idea that consumers will favour products that offer the most quality, performance and features and that the organisation should therefore devote its energy to making continuous product improvements.

Attention to product quality will result in greater profitability (e.g. more sales). Consumers will favour those products that offer the most quality, performance or innovative features. Managers in product-oriented organisations focus their energy on making superior products and improving them over time

This philosophy is summed up in the phrase *"If a man can write a better book, preach a better sermon or build a better mousetrap, though he builds his house in the woods, the world will make a beaten path to his door."* Attributed to Ralph Waldo Emerson, 1889.

3. THE SELLING CONCEPT
The selling concept is the idea that consumers, if left alone, will ordinarily not buy enough of the organisation's products. The organisation must therefore undertake an aggressive selling and promotion effort.
When what can be supplied is equal or greater than what is demanded, profit (sales) can be improved by selling more The firm should sell what it makes rather than make (based on customer needs) what it can sell
   1. This concept is typically practised with unsought goods, those that buyers do not normally think of buying i.e. encyclopaedias, kitchen utensils
   2. The selling concept is also practised in the non-profit area; for example, "selling" a political candidate

Dominant era: 1920's to Mid 1930's, W.W.II to early 1950's

4. THE MARKETING CONCEPT
The marketing concepts holds that when what can be supplied is greater than what will be demanded and there is intense competition among suppliers, the key to achieving organisational goals (profit, sales) consists in determining and satisfying the needs and wants of target markets and delivering the desired satisfactions more effectively and efficiently than competitors do. Marketing strategies must be based on known customer needs.

THE MARKETING CONCEPT

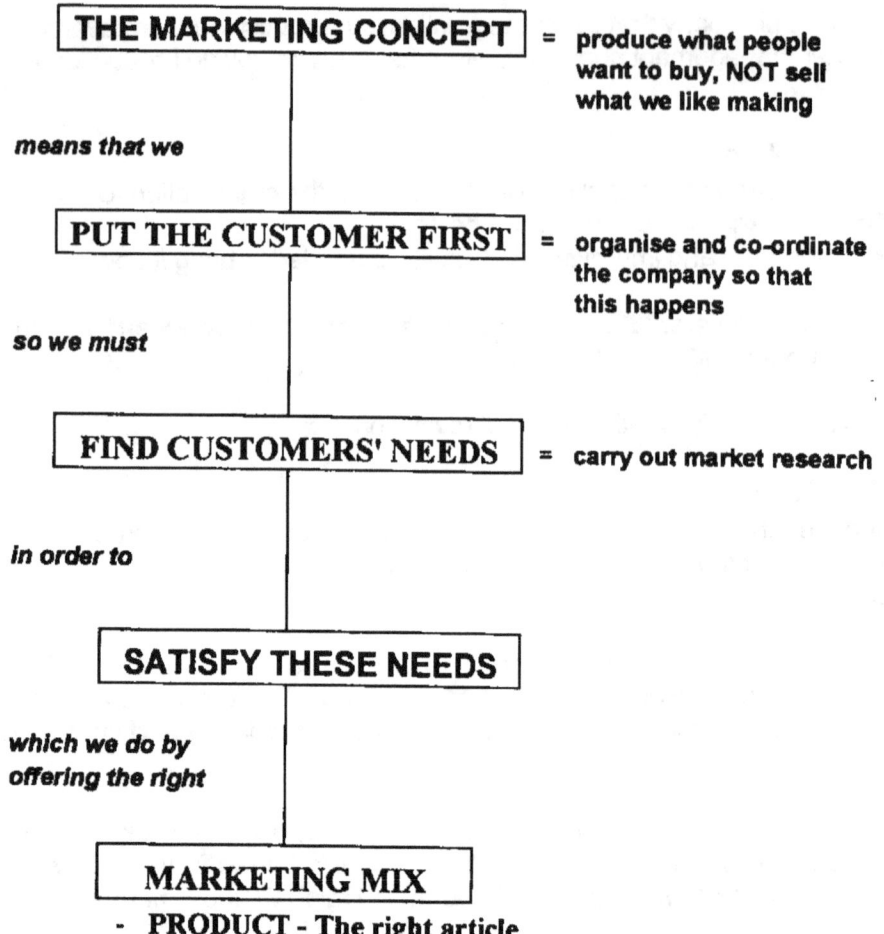

Contrasting the selling and marketing concept:
- The Selling Concept takes an inside-out perspective-looking at the company's needs and wants in terms of existing products and ways to find customers for them
- The Marketing Concept takes an outside-in perspective - identifying the needs and wants of a clearly defined market and adjusting company efforts to make products that meet the needs.

Dominant era: 1930's to W.W.II 1950's to present.

"I do not consider a sale complete until goods are worn out and the customer still satisfied. We will thank anyone to return goods that are not perfectly satisfactory. Above all things we wish to avoid is having a dissatisfied customer" LL Bean in his first circular 1912.

John B McKitterick, President of General Electric, 1957, referring to marketing when addressing the AMA said: *"It is a customer oriented, integrated, profit oriented philosophy of business."*

To illustrate the marketing era concept Peter Drucker, in 1954, said: *"if we want to know what business is, we must first start with its purpose... There is only one valid definition of business purpose: to create a customer. What business thinks it produces is not of first importance - especially not to the future of the business or to its success. What the customer thinks he/she is buying, what he/she considers "value" is decisive - it determines what a business is, what it produces and whether it will prosper"* Peter Drucker, The Practice of Management, 1954

The need to make a profit however remains despite all efforts to satisfy consumer needs i.e. **"meeting customer needs profitably"** for the organisation

The Strategic Marketing Concept
The strategic marketing concepts holds that when what can be supplied is greater than what will be demanded, the key to achieving organisational goals consists in determining and satisfying the needs and wants of target markets more effectively and efficiently than competitors i.e.
- the firm must satisfy customer needs while sustaining a competitive advantage to ensure long term profitability
- have both a customer orientation and a competitor orientation

5. SOCIETAL MARKETING CONCEPT
The societal marketing concept holds that the organisation's task is to determine the needs, wants and interests of target markets and to deliver the desired satisfactions more effectively and efficiently than competitors in a way that preserves or enhances the consumer's and society's well-being. It focuses on other stakeholders, as well as the business and its customers. The societal marketing concept recognises the need to balance 3 items:
1. Company profits
2. Customer wants
3. Society's interests

The difference between short-term consumer wants and long-term consumer welfare is taken into consideration when designing marketing strategy. Examples of a companies adopting the Societal concept:
- Gheissa Dolphin Safe Tuna - Actually more expensive than regular tuna, but is more appealing due to society's concerns.
- Body Shop - Refilling of empty containers

We are now still essentially in the marketing concept era, since that is the dominant concept, but increasing pressure is being put on to companies to adopt the societal concept.

Importance of the Marketing Concept
According to the Customer Service Institute, it costs as much as five times as much to acquire a new customer than it does to service an existing one. Customers tell twice as many people about a bad experience over a good one. According to the American Marketing Association (AMA), for an average company, 65% of its business comes from its presently satisfied customers.

IMPLEMENTING THE MARKETING CONCEPT
To implement the marketing concept, an organization must accept some general conditions and recognize and deal with several problems. Consequently, the marketing concept has yet to be fully accepted by all businesses.
1. To implement the marketing concept, management must first establish an information system that will enable the firm to learn about customers' needs and use the information to create satisfying products. Without an adequate information system, an organization cannot be customer-oriented.

2. Management's second major task for implementing the marketing concept is to coordinate all activities. This may require restructuring operations and objectives.
3. Effective implementation of the marketing concept also requires a market orientation—the organizationwide generation of market intelligence pertaining to current and future customer needs, dissemination of the intelligence across departments, and organizationwide responsiveness to it.
4. Achieving the full profit potential of each customer relationship should be the fundamental goal of every marketing strategy. At the most basic level, profits can be obtained through relationships in the following ways:
   a. Acquiring new customers
   b. Enhancing the profitability of existing customers
   c. Extending the duration of customer relationships

THE GOALS OF THE MARKETING SYSTEM

- **Maximise Consumption** This goal uses promotions and advertising to stimulate demand and consumption. The idea is that the greater the level of consumption, the better things are for both the consumer and the seller.
- **Maximise Consumer Satisfaction** This goal stresses the quality of the consumer's consumptive experience over its sheer volume. The idea is that marketing ultimately succeeds only if consumers are satisfied with products they consume
- **Maximise Choice** This goal strives to increase the selection and availability of products to expand the consumer's choice among alternatives. Ideally, this goal of the marketing system would generate product forms to suit every imaginable manifestation of consumer wants and needs.
- **Maximise Life Quality** This goal corresponds to the societal marketing concept's view that the marketing system must address the needs of the many as well as the needs of the few.

MARKETING CHALLENGES IN THE NEXT CENTURY

- **Rapid Globalisation** Technological and economic developments continue to shrink the distances between countries.
- **The Changing World Economy** Even as new markets open to rising affluence in such countries as the "newly industrialised" pacific rim, poverty in many areas and slowed economies in previously industrial nations has already changed the world economy.
- **The Call for More Ethics and Social Responsibility** The greed of the 1980s and the problems caused by pollution in Eastern Europe and elsewhere has spurred a new interest in ethical conduct in business
- **The New Marketing Landscape** The new marketing landscape is a dynamic, fast-paced and evolving function of all these changes and opportunities. More than ever, there is no static formula for success.

NATURE OF MARKETING AND MARKETING MANAGEMENT

There are a number of digressions on what a marketing manager actually does.
- The simplest view is that a marketing manager is simply someone who plans and implements a series of marketing activities.
- Somewhat more broadly however, a marketing manager is someone who can utilize marketing principles, theories and analytical techniques to solve marketing problems.

A marketing Problem could be:
- Development of an annual marketing plan.
- Development of a new product and a program for its market introduction.
- Determine the cause of an adverse trend such as declining sales and develop a marketing program to reverse the trend.

MARKETING MANAGEMENT

TOPIC: THE MARKETING ENVIRONMENT
LECTURE: 2

THE MARKETING ENVIRONMENT

A company's marketing environment consists of the actors and forces outside marketing that affect marketing management's ability to develop and maintain successful transactions with its target customers.

Marketing Environment (def) - all factors that may affect an organisation directly or indirectly.

Environmental factors affect organisations and organisations affect their environment. The marketing environment offers both opportunities and threats. Companies must use their marketing research and intelligence systems to watch the changing environment and must adapt their marketing strategies to environmental trends and developments.

The marketing environment consists of a microenvironment and a macroenvironment.

The microenvironment consists of the forces close to the company that affect its ability to serve its customers - the company, suppliers, marketing channel firms, customer markets, competitors and publics. The macroenvironment consists of the larger societal forces that affect the whole microenvironment - demographic, economic, natural, technological, political and cultural forces.

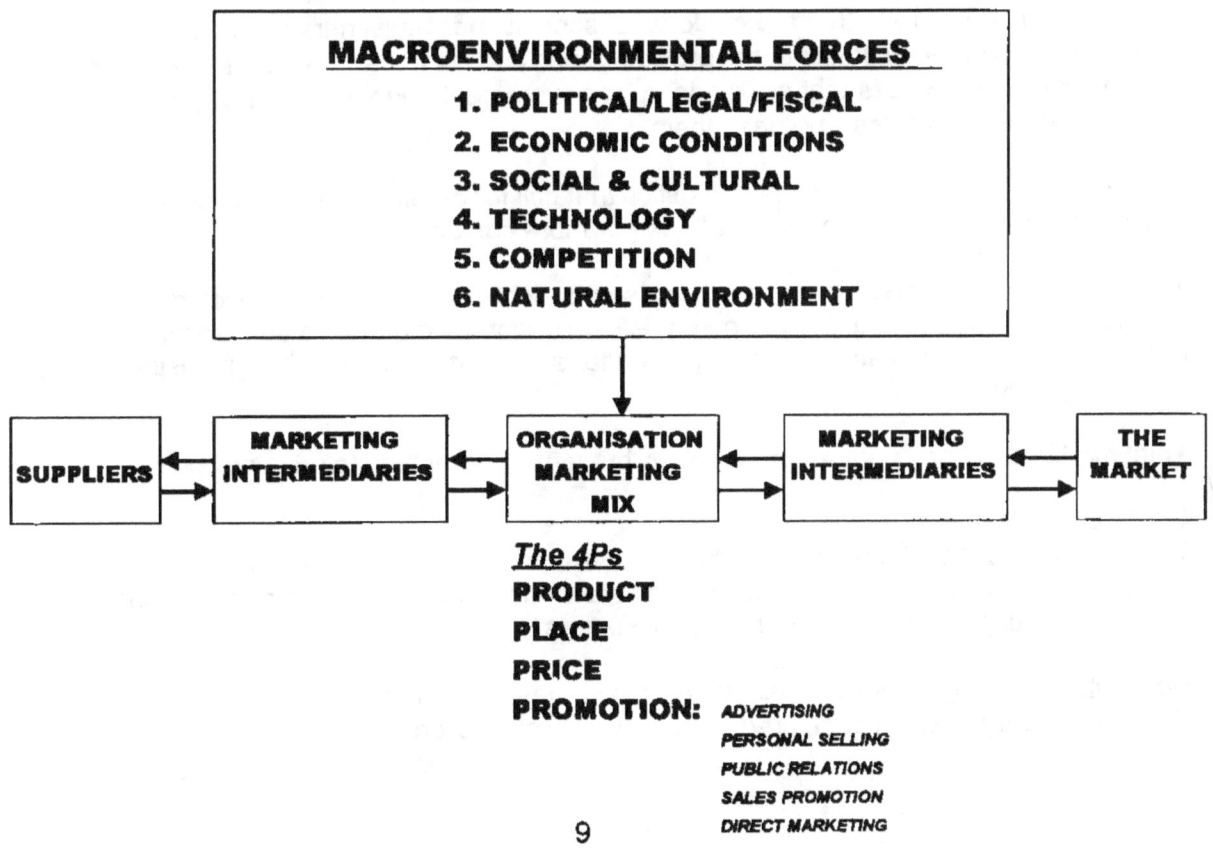

THE COMPANY'S MICROENVIRONMENT

THE COMPANY
In designing marketing plans, marketing management should take other company functions, such as top management, finance, research and development, purchasing, manufacturing, human resources and accounting, into consideration. All these interrelated groups form the internal environment.

SUPPLIERS
Suppliers are firms and individuals that provide the resources needed by the company to produce its goods and services. Supplier developments can seriously affect marketing. Marketing managers must therefore watch supply availability. Supply shortages or delays, labour strikes and other events can cost sales in the short run and damage customer goodwill in the long run.

MARKETING INTERMEDIARIES
Marketing intermediaries are firms that help the company to promote, sell and distribute its goods to final buyers. They include middlemen, physical distribution firms, marketing services agencies and financial intermediaries. Middlemen are distribution channel firms that help the company find customers or make sales to them. These include wholesalers and retailers who buy and resell merchandise.

CUSTOMERS
The company must study its customer market(s) closely. Consumer markets consist of
- **Individuals and households** that buy goods and services for personal consumption.
- **Business markets** that buy goods and services for further processing or for use in their production process.
- **Reseller markets** that buy goods and services to resell at a profit.
- **Institutional markets** that are made up of schools, hospitals, nursing homes, prisons and other institutions that provide goods and services to people in their care.
- **Government markets** that are made up of government agencies that buy goods and services for others who need them.

Each market type has special characteristics that call for careful study by the seller. At any point in time, the firm may deal with one or more customer markets.

The total market demand for a product or a service is the total volume that would be bought by a defined consumer group in a defined geographic area in a defined time period in a defined marketing environment under a defined level and mix of industry marketing effort.

Total market demand is not a fixed number, but a function of the stated conditions.

COMPETITORS
The marketing concept states that to be successful, a company must satisfy the needs and wants of consumers better than its competitors do. Thus, marketers must do more than simply adapt to the needs of target consumers.

No single marketing strategy is best for all companies. Each firm must consider its own size and industry position compared to those of its competitors.

Large firms with dominant positions in the industry can use certain strategies that smaller firms cannot afford.

COMPETITIVE FACTORS

1. The Nature of Competition
Four competitive environments.
- **Absolute monopoly** - one seller (e.g. public utilities).
- **.Oligopoly** - a few large sellers dominate the market (e.g. auto industry).
- **Monopolistic competition** - many sellers with none large enough to dominate the market; slight difference in product (e.g. shampoo).
- **Pure competition** - large numbers of sellers with identical products (e.g. farm commodities).

2. Entry and Exit of Competing Firms.
- Firms examine changes in competition by looking at firms entering and leaving the market.
- Barriers to entry include scarcity of raw materials and structural barriers.

3. Major Strategic Changes by Competitors

PUBLICS
The company's marketing environment also includes various publics. A public is any group that has an actual or potential interest or impact on an organisation's ability to achieve its objectives. There are seven types of publics

1. Financial Publics
Influence the company's ability to obtain funds. Banks, investment houses and stockholders are the principal financial publics.

2. Media Publics
are those that carry news, features and editorial opinion. They include newspapers, magazines and radio and television stations.

3. Government Publics
Management must take government developments into account. Marketers must often consult the company's lawyers on issues of product safety, truth-in-advertising and other matters.

4. Citizen-Action Publics
A company's marketing decisions may be questioned by consumer organisations, environmental groups, minority groups and other pressure groups. Its publics relations department can help it stay in touch with consumer and citizen groups.

5. Local Publics
Every company has local publics, such as neighbourhood residents and community organisations. Large companies usually appoint community-relations officer to deal with the community, attend meetings, answer questions and contribute to worthwhile causes.

6. General Public
A company needs to be concerned about the general public's attitude toward its products and activities. The public's image of the company affects its buying. Thus, many large corporations invest huge sums of money to promote and build a healthy corporate image.

7. Internal Publics
A company's internal publics include its workers, managers and the board of directors. Large companies use newsletters and other means to inform and motivate their internal publics. When employees feel good about their company, this positive attitude spills over to their external publics.

THE COMPANY'S MACROENVIRONMENT

Marketing does not occur in a vacuum. The marketing environment consists of external uncontrollable forces that directly and/or indirectly impact the organisation.

Environmental change is inevitable. Changes in the environment create opportunities and threats for the organisations.

1. DEMOGRAPHIC FORCES
Demography is the study of human populations in terms of size, density, location, age, gender, race, occupation and other statistics. The demographic environment is of considerable interest to marketers because it involves people and people make up markets.

Amongst the most important demographic characteristics are
- Population size and growth trends e.g. Birth & death rate
- Changing age structure of the population e.g. Ageing population
- Geographical distribution of population, density, mobility trends
- The changing family e.g. marriages, divorces, single parents, smaller families, fewer children, the rise of non-family households, increasing age of those marrying, delayed child-bearing, increased two-income families
- Rising number of educated people
- Racial, ethnic & religious structure of population

2. ECONOMIC FORCES
The economic environment consists of factors that affect consumer purchasing power and spending patterns. These include:
1. Income and the New Economic Realities
    - The "affluent society"
    - Disposable personal income - (def) consumer's total after tax income to be used for spending and savings.
2. Inflation - (def) a general rise in prices that people must pay for goods and services.
3. Productivity (def) - an estimate of output per labour hour worked.
    - Increased productivity allows wages to rise without raising prices.
4. Unemployment.
- New global arrangements, automation, computerisation, robotisation, and mergers and acquisitions have led to downsizing.
- Unemployment affects marketers because it reduces buying power.

Marketers need to be aware of the following predominant economic trends.

- **Income distribution and changes in purchasing power**

Where consumer purchasing power is reduced, as in an economic recession, value-for-money becomes a key purchasing criterion. Marketers must pursue value-based marketing to capture and retain price conscious customers during lean economic times, unlike boom periods when consumers become addicted to personal consumption.

- **Changing consumer spending patterns**

Changes in chief economic variables such as income, cost of living, interest rates and savings and borrowing patterns have a large impact on the marketplace. Companies watch these variables by using economic forecasting.

3. NATURAL ENVIRONMENT
Examples: drought, floods, severe winter

The natural environment involves the natural resources that are needed as inputs by marketers or that are affected by marketing activities. Environmental concerns have grown steadily during the past two decades. Protection of the natural environment will remain a crucial worldwide issue facing business and the public. Marketers should be aware of the four trends in the natural environment :
- shortages of raw materials
- increased cost of energy
- increased pollution
- government intervention in natural resource management

4. TECHNOLOGICAL ENVIRONMENT
The technological environment is perhaps the most dramatic force now shaping our destiny. Technology has released such wonders as penicillin, organ transplants and computers. It has also released such horrors as nerve gas and the nuclear bomb. Our attitude towards technology depends on whether we are more impressed with its wonders or its blunders. Every new technology replaces an older technology. When old industries fought or ignored new technologies, their businesses declined.

New technologies create new markets and opportunities. The marketer should watch the following trends in technology.
- fast pace of technological change
- higher R & D budgets
- concentration on minor improvements
- increased regulation
- impact of the Internet

5. POLITICAL/LEGAL ENVIRONMENT
Marketing decisions are strongly affected by developments in the political environment. The political environment consists of laws, government agencies and pressure groups that influence and limit various organisations and individuals in a given society.

a. **Legislation regulating business.** Some government rules and regulations are essential for the organisation and monitoring of the marketplace.

The Government intervenes in two modes:
- Regulation of marketing conduct.
- Regulation of marketing institutions and industry structure.

e.g. Anti – monopoly laws, Consumer protection legislation

b. Growth of public interest groups e.g.

CONSUMERISM - the movement to aid and protect consumers from business practices that infringe upon their rights.
- Marketers responses to consumerism: opposing it, ignoring it or responding to improve the buyer - seller relationship.
- Government responses to consumerism: consumer protection and consumer education.

ECOLOGICAL MOVEMENT - Public opinion, laws, competitiveness and social responsibility are making companies more attentive to ecological factors. Ecological environmentalism is expected to be a major global force in the 1990's.
Ecology - (def) the science of the relationship between living things and their environment.

Informal laws of ecology are important to marketers.
1. Everything is connected to everything else.
2. Everything must go somewhere.
3. Nature knows best.
4. Anything of importance has a cost.

c. Increased emphasis on ethics and socially responsible actions - society becomes concerned about marketers actions when those actions are questionable.

6. SOCIOCULTURAL ENVIRONMENT

The cultural environment is made up of institutions and other forces that affect society's values, perceptions, preferences and behaviours. People grow up in a particular society that shapes their basic beliefs and values. They absorb a world view that defines their relationships to themselves and others. Core beliefs and values are relatively enduring. Products that conflict with core values are unlikely to be adopted.

The following characteristics can affect marketing decision because they establish the limits regarding acceptable decisions. Marketers must be aware of these cultural influences and how they vary across societies within the markets served by the firm.

- **Persistence of cultural values.** People's core beliefs and values have a high degree of persistence.

- **Shifts in secondary cultural values.** Although core values are fairly persistent, cultural swings do take place. Consider the impact of music groups, etc. Marketers want to predict cultural shifts in order to spot new opportunities or threats.

- **People's views of themselves.** People vary in their emphasis on serving themselves and serving others. Some people seek personal pleasure, wanting fun, change and escape. Others seek self-realisation through religion, recreation etc. People use products, brands and services as a means of self-expression and buy products and services that match their views of themselves.

ENVIRONMENTAL SCANNING & ANALYSIS

To track these external forces a company uses environmental scanning and analysis which is a continual monitoring of what is going on. Marketing decision - makers must collect, analyse and diagnose information on the external environment.

1. Collecting the information

Environmental scanning collects information about external forces. It is conducted through the Marketing Information System (which will be discussed further in later lectures). Environmental Scanning may include formal or informal techniques

> **Environmental Scanning** – (def) the process of collecting information about forces in the marketing environment.

2. Analysing the information

Environmental Analysis - Identifying opportunities and threats by:
1. Evaluating attractiveness of environmental forces.
2. Identifying opportunities and threats.
3. Realistically evaluating the environment and its impact on the firm.

Environmental analysis determines environmental changes and predicts future changes in the environment. The marketing manager should be able to determine possible threats and opportunities from the changing environment. This will help avoid crisis management.

> **Environmental Analysis** – (def) the process of assessing and interpreting the information gathered through environmental scanning

3. Making marketing decisions: Environmental Diagnosis.

Organisations must plan a response to environmental factors.
- Reactive organisations react to innovations.

Reactive response – Changing the marketing mix in response to environmental changes (Most common type of response).

- Proactive organisations take purposeful action to meet challenges or create marketing opportunities.

Proactive response - Trying to change the environment. e.g. lobbying.

> **Environmental Diagnosis** - (def) the process of making marketing decisions by assessing the significance of threats or opportunities.

Marketers must be prepared for changing environmental conditions. A marketing-oriented firm looks outward to the environment in which it operates adapting to take advantage of emerging opportunities and to minimise potential threats.

Two key decisions that management need to make are what to scan and how to organise the activity. Clearly in theory every event in the world has the potential to affect a company's operations, but to establish a scanning system which covers every conceivable force would be unmanageable.

The first task then, is to define a feasible range of forces that require monitoring. These are the potentially relevant environmental forces that have the most likelihood of affecting future business prospects.

The second prerequisite for an effective scanning system is to design a system which provides a fast response to events that are only partially predictable and emerge as surprises and grow very quickly.

A complete environmental scanning system should perform the following:
1. Monitor trends, issues and events and study their implications.
2. Develop forecasts, scenarios and issues analysis as input to strategic decision-making.
3. Provide a focal point for the interpretation and analysis of environmental information identified by other people in the company.
4. Establish a library or database for environmental information.
5. Provide a group of internal experts on external affairs.
6. Disseminate information on the business environment through newsletters, reports and lectures.
7. Evaluate and revise the scanning system itself by applying ew tools and procedures.

The benefits of formal environmental scanning are believed to be:
1. Better general awareness of and responsiveness to environmental changes
2. Better decision-making.
3. Greater effectiveness in dealing with the government.
4. Improved industry and market analysis.
5. Better foreign investment and international marketing.
6. Improved resource allocation and diversification decisions
7. Superior planning.

MARKETING MANAGEMENT

TOPIC: STRATEGIC PLANNING
LECTURE: 3

STRATEGIC PLANNING

To meet changing conditions in their industries, companies need to look ahead and develop long-term strategies. Marketing plays an important role in strategic planning since it provides information and other inputs to help prepare the strategic plan. Also, strategic planning defines marketing's role in the organisation.

It is necessary to discuss strategic market planning and marketing early in the course. A strategic marketing plan gives direction to a firm's efforts and better enables it to understand the dimensions of marketing research, consumer analysis and product, distribution, promotion and price planning which will be discussed in later lectures.

Planning is something we do in advance of taking action, i.e.:
- it is anticipatory decision making
- it is required when the future state that we desire involves a set of interdependent decisions
- it is a process that is directed toward producing one or more future states which are desired and which are not expected to occur unless action Is taken

A strategy describes the direction an organisation will pursue within its chosen environment, and guides the allocation of resources. A strategy also provides the logic that integrates the parochial perspectives of functional departments and operating units and points them in the same direction.

Strategic Planning is the process of developing and maintaining a strategic fit between an organisation's goals and capabilities and its changing marketing opportunities

The aim of strategic planning is to reshape and shape the company's businesses and product so that they combine to produce satisfactory profits and growth.

Strategic planning requires a general marketing orientation rather than a narrow functional orientation. All functional areas must include marketing and must be co-ordinated to reach organisational goals. It is a hierarchical process, from company wide to marketing specific. (Marketing concept, implemented from top down.)

Most large companies consist of four organizational levels which are:
1. **Corporate**
2. **Business unit**
3. **Product**

Planning responsibilities
1. **Corporate** - responsible for designing a corporate strategic plan to guide the whole enterprise
2. **Business unit** - develops a business unit strategic plan to carry the business unit into a profitable future.
3. **Product level** - (product lines, brands etc.) - develops marketing plans for achieving objectives in its markets.

CORPORATE AND MARKETING PLANNING

There is some argument as to the relationship between corporate planning and marketing planning. The two extreme views are:
- the two forms of planning are synonymous
- the role of marketing in corporate planning is no different from that of other functional areas in a business - it is merely a functional plan.

Marketing oriented organisations take the view that the marketing plan lies at the heart of a company's revenue earning activities. It is not possible, therefore, to plan a company's marketing activities in isolation from other business functions. Consequently, the marketing planning process should be firmly based in a total corporate planning system.

The corporate planning process must begin with the setting of corporate objectives followed by strategies and plans for each separate function in the organisation.

The Nature and Scope of Business Planning

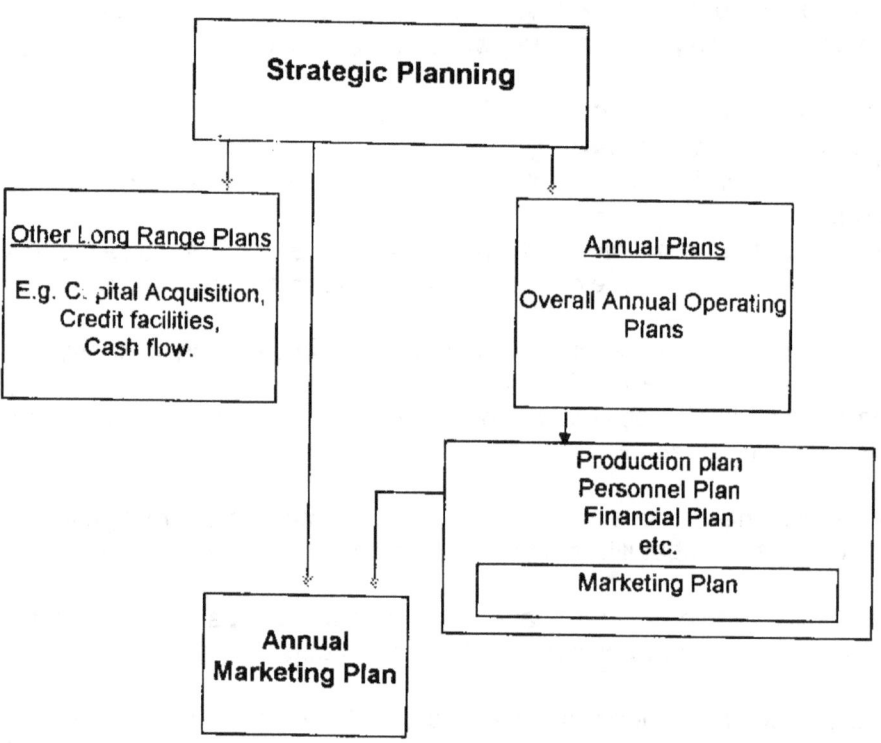

Corporate objectives need to be communicated throughout the company as do the individual functional objectives. The key step in the marketing planning process is the setting of marketing objectives and the strategies to achieve them. Marketing objectives should be understandable, achievable, capable of being measured and communicated to and agreed by all concerned and be derived from corporate level objectives.

The purpose of the corporate plan is to achieve a clear statement of:
1. **Where the company is now** Identification and analysis of the key environmental, economic, commercial, political, social and technological trends. Also an assessment of the current health of the company in capital employed, turnover, key markets, market share, etc.
2. **Where the company intends to go** This may be expressed in terms of capital employed, the return on capital employed, etc.
3. **How it will organise its resources in order to get there** What strategies the company intends to follow in order to achieve its objectives.

THE 5 STEPS OF THE CORPORATE PLANNING PROCESS

1. **The statement of corporate objectives.** This is often expressed in terms of turnover, profit before tax and return on assets from a quantitative perspective. Qualitative corporate objectives relate to image, stance, positioning, corporate citizenship and conduct. These objectives should be consistent with the company's mission statement.

2. **The management audit** - a systematic appraisal of the business environment and the company's operations.

3. **The development of separate objectives and strategies with broad resource implications for each business function within the planning horizon used in the company.** This must take account of the analyses made in the management audit, so that they are based on the most realistic assessments available to the company. It is important that the objectives and strategies of each function are carefully integrated, and this will be one of the major responsibilities of corporate management. In this way, corporate planning involves a 'top down' and 'bottom' up planning process.

4. **Detailed plans for each function for a shorter time span, often one year.** These will set out the actions, responsibilities, timing and costs heeded to achieve the first year's objectives.

5. **Development of the corporate plan.** In step five, these plans will be merged into the corporate plan.

A well conceived corporate plan is a long term vision of what the company is now and is hence striving to become - taking account of shareholder expectations, environmental and market trends and the distinctive competence of the company as revealed by the management audit.

A corporate plan must be based on sound information and be developed in an orderly, competent way. It must also be reviewed and updated regularly. It can then be the source of stability in turbulent conditions which allows change to be managed without incurring a constant sense of crisis.

STRATEGIC MARKET PLANS

A Strategic Market Plan is an outline of the methods and resources needed to achieve a firm's goals in a specific target market(s).

It takes into account not only marketing, but also all functional aspects of a business unit that must be co-ordinated, including production, finance and human resources as well as environmental issues.

The strategic market planning process is based on an analysis of the environment.
> 1. Marketers differ in their viewpoints about the effect of environmental variables on marketing planning strategy.
> 2. When environmental variables affect an organisation's overall goals, resources, opportunities or marketing objectives, they also affect its marketing strategies, which are based on these factors.

Plans must be feasible and respond to changes in the business environment.

THE MARKETING PLAN
The process of strategic market planning yields a marketing strategy that is the framework for a marketing plan, which is **a written document that specifies the activities to be performed to implement and control an organisation's marketing activities**.

The set of marketing strategies that are implemented and used at the same time is referred to as the organisation's **marketing program**.

ESTABLISHING AN ORGANIZATIONAL MISSION AND GOALS
The goals of an organisation should be derived from its mission. The mission statement describes the long-term view or vision, of what the organisation wants to become.

THE MISSION STATEMENT defines the intended future role and purpose of the organisation. and is expressed in terms of:
- the business the organisation is in
- the type of customer it wishes to serve
- the specific needs of these customers
- the means by which it will serve the needs
- the philosophy of doing business

A mission statement should include a firm's distinctive competency, which is something that it does extremely well, sometimes so well that it gives the company an advantage over its competition. The focus, therefore, is on what the company does best and its competitive advantage in relation to competitors.

> "The railroads were in trouble not because the need was filled by others, but because it was not filled by the railroads themselves. They let others take customers away from them because they assumed themselves to be in the railroad business rather than the transportation business."
> (Theodore Levitt in "Marketing Myopia")

Having a mission statement can benefit the organisation by:
a. Giving the organisation a clear purpose and direction
b. Describing the unique focus of the organisation that helps to differentiate it from competitors
c. Keeping the organisation focused on customer needs rather than its own abilities
d. Providing specific direction and guidelines to top managers for selecting from among alternative courses of action
e. Providing guidance to all employees and managers of an organisation, even if they work in different parts of the world

ORGANIZATIONAL GOALS & OBJECTIVES
An organisation's **GOALS**, which are derived from its mission, guide the remainder of its planning efforts.
1. Goals focus on the end results sought by the organisation.
2. Organizations can have short-term and long-term goals

OBJECTIVES should be Specific, Measurable, Attainable, Realistic and Timed-out (SMART)

DEVELOPING CORPORATE AND BUSINESS-UNIT STRATEGIES

In any organisation there are essentially three levels of strategic market planning:
1. **Corporate Strategy,**
2. **Business-Unit Strategy**
3. **Marketing Strategy.**

The outcomes of each planning stage must be consistent with the stage that precedes it.

1. CORPORATE STRATEGY

CORPORATE STRATEGY determines the means for utilising resources in the areas of production, finance, research and development, human resources and marketing to reach the organisation's goals.

1. It determines the scope of the business, its resource deployment and competitive advantages and overall marketing co-ordination of production, finance, marketing and other functional areas.

2. It applies to all organisations, not just corporations.

3. Corporate strategy planners are concerned with
    a. Issues such as diversification, competition, differentiation, interrelationships between business units and environmental issues
    b. Attempting to match the resources of the organisation with the opportunities and risks in the environment
    c. Defining the scope and role of the strategic business units of the firm so that they are co-ordinated to reach the ends desired

4. One of the most helpful tools proposed to aid corporate managers in their planning efforts is product-portfolio analysis, the **Boston Consulting Group (BCG)** approach, which is based on the philosophy that a product's market growth rate and its relative market share are important considerations in determining marketing strategy. The BCG approach integrates all the firm's products into a single, overall matrix and evaluates them to determine appropriate strategies for individual SBUs and the overall portfolio strategies.

BUSINESS PORTFOLIO: the collection of businesses and products that make up the company

---
PORTFOLIO ANALYSIS: a tool by which management identifies and evaluates the various businesses that make up the company

---
PRODUCT PORTFOLIO ANALYSIS: analysing a firm's individual products as though they are a collection of separate investments

---
STRATEGIC BUSINESS UNIT (SBU)
- a unit of the company that has a separate mission and objectives and that can be planned independently from other company businesses;
- a division, product line or other profit centre within the parent company

Note: an SBU can be a company division, a product line within a division or a single product or brand. The SBU is used to define areas for consideration in a specific strategic market plan.

THE BCG GROWTH-SHARE MATRIX is based on the philosophy that a product's growth rate and relative market share are important considerations in strategy
- **IDEA**: Fund the growth of promising new products from profits of established products
- **ASSUMPTION**: Market share increases result in profit increases (Note: this assumption is an interesting idea and can be useful as a guide to understanding strategy, but many do not accept this assumption.)

BCG GROWTH-SHARE MATRIX

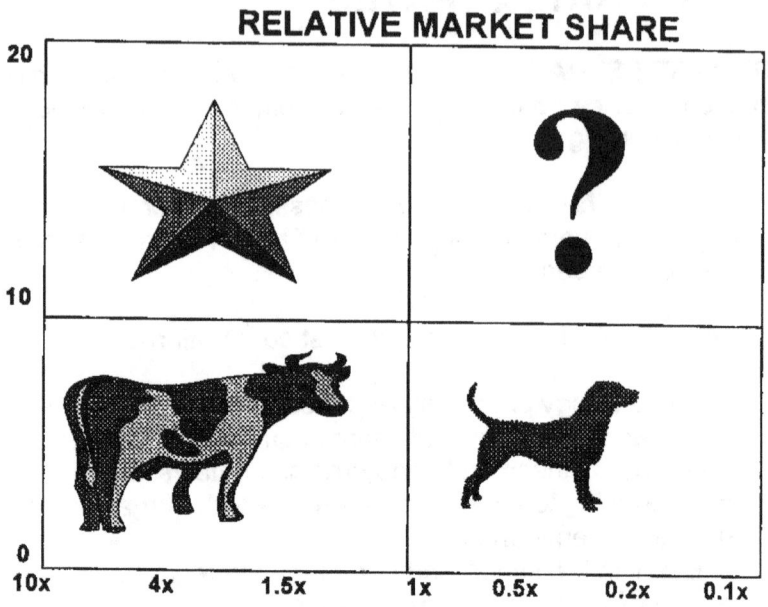

Definitions:
- **MARKET GROWTH RATE**: the annual rate of growth of the specific market or industry in which a given SBU is competing
- **RELATIVE MARKET SHARE**: sales of the SBU divided by the sales of the largest firm in the industry
- **STRATEGIC BUSINESS UNIT**: (SBU) separate profit centres in an organisation, treated as though each is a separate, independent business

STARS: products which have a relatively high market share in a high growth industry.
    Assumption: if we still have a relatively high market share when the market is saturated (industry growth stagnates), then we will have relatively high profits in the industry; it will be expensive for competitors to take sales (Market Share) away from us. It is, therefore, worth while to inject funds into building star products.

QUESTION MARKS or PROBLEM CHILDREN: products which show promise due to high industry growth, but which have relatively low market share within that industry.
    Assumption: we will have to use the profits of other products in the portfolio to build the market share of this product so that it will have relatively high market share by the time industry growth slows. This might be difficult and too costly to be worthwhile.

DOGS: products with low relative market share in low a growth industry
    Assumption: that we are at a competitive disadvantage in that it would be very difficult and costly to gain sales by increasing Market Share

CASH COWS: products which have reached market dominance (high relative market share) in a market in which industry growth is slow or stagnant.

Assumption: relatively high market share correlates with relatively high profits. Since it is more costly for competitors to take Market Share away from us than for us to maintain high Market Share, we have higher profits. Cash cows generate high profits which are used to build rising stars or problem children.

> **NOTE** that the idea behind portfolio analysis from the BCG perspective is to fund the growth of promising new product development and launch from the profits of successful products in the portfolio of products.
> The long-term health of an organisation depends on this.

Decisions regarding which SBU to:
1. **Build** - increase the SBUs market share through injections of cash - even though this might affect short term profits
2. **Hold / Maintain** the SBUs market share without appreciably altering the cash that it uses
3. **Harvest** - increase the SBUs short-term cash output, even if this results in a loss of market share
4. **Divest** - sell the SBU to put its cash, physical and human resources to use elsewhere in the firm

5. Another tool used is **THE GE BUSINESS-PLANNING GRID**

This matrix, which is an attempt to improve on the BCG matrix, uses two dimensions of three zones (High, Medium, Low) each:

- **Industry attractiveness** is an index made up of market size, market growth, industry profit margin, amount of competition, seasonality & cyclicality of demand, and industry cost structure.
- **Business strength** is an index of relative market share, price, competitiveness, product quality, customer & market knowledge, sales effectiveness, and geographic advantages.

THE GE BUSINESS-PLANNING GRID

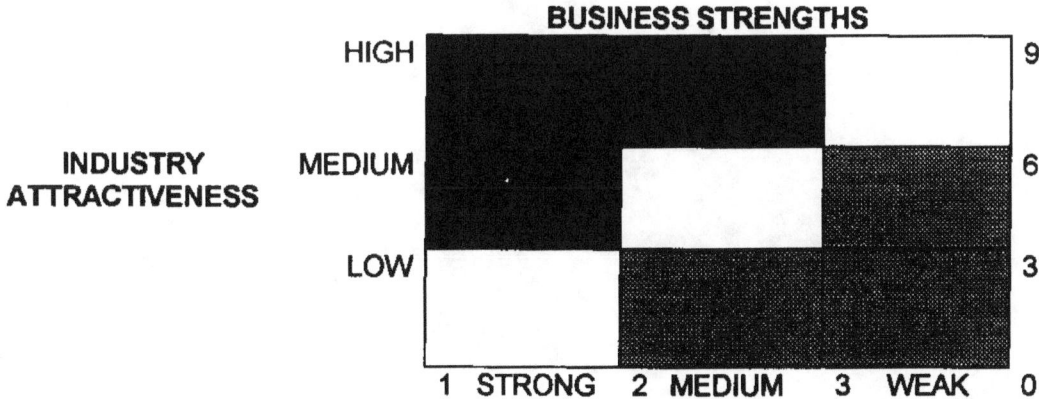

2. BUSINESS-UNIT STRATEGY

The next step in strategic market planning is to determine business directions and develop business-unit strategies. A business may choose one or more competitive strategies

1. **MARKET PENETRATION** is a strategy of increasing sales in current markets with current products.

2. **MARKET DEVELOPMENT** is a strategy of increasing sales of current products in new markets.

3. **PRODUCT DEVELOPMENT** is a strategy of increasing sales by improving present products or developing new products for current markets.

4. **DIVERSIFICATION** is a strategy of increasing sales by selling new products to new markets.

The ANSOFF MATRIX

	EXISTING PRODUCT	NEW PRODUCT
EXISTING MARKET	MARKET PENETRATION	PRODUCT DEVELOPMENT
NEW MARKET	MARKET DEVELOPMENT	DIVERSIFICATION

MARKETING MANAGEMENT

TOPIC: MARKETING PLANNING
LECTURE: 4

MARKETING PLANNING

Marketing plans may take a variety of forms ranging from verbal intentions to a set of budgets for achievement, through to formalised structures and procedures used as part of the corporate planning process. In many organisations in the commercial and non-commercial world they may not even exist.

Marketing planning must be recognised as a management process - which means effective systems for organising, directing, controlling, co-ordinating and evaluating cannot be ignored. Like any planning system, the user must be clear on the intended use and the contribution desired, otherwise implementation of the plan will result in disappointment and frustration.

The marketing planner must ask certain fundamental questions:
1. Do we have the ability to match our ambitions? (Often ambition to achieve a marketing planning system reaches beyond the realities of ability)
2. Have we considered the planning horizons in terms of time?
3. Have we defined the boundaries to the system clearly?
4. What purposes are to be served by the marketing planning system? (This will help later to determine objectives).
5. What structure should exist to enable the plan to be planned, implemented and achieved?
6. What do we require to achieve the purpose we have now identified?
7. What constraints currently limit our ability, and can these, be overcome?
8. What contributions are we seeking to organisational performance from the plan?

Like all planning, marketing planning concerns the future. It is our approach to the future which is important. The future involves a time dimension which needs to be clearly specified and depends on a clear understanding of the organisational and market needs.

Marketing planning means change. It is a process of deciding currently what to do in the future with a full appreciation of our resource position, the need to set clear communicable, measurable objectives; the development of alternative courses of action and a means of assessing the best route towards the achievement of specified objectives.

THE BENEFITS OF MARKETING PLANNING
Marketing planning is designed to assist the process of marketing decision, making under prevailing conditions of risk and uncertainty. Above all, the process of marketing planning has a number of benefits:
- motivates staff
- secures participation and involvement
- achieves commitment
- leads ultimately to better decision making
- requires management staff collectively to make clear judgmental statements about assumptions - the very basis upon which the future depends
- ensures that a systematic approach to the future has been taken

- prevents short-termism, the tendency to place all effort on the 'here and now'
- creates a climate in which change can be made and in which standards for performance can he established
- enables a control system to be designed and established, whereby performance can be assessed against predetermined criteria.

Marketing plans can be both strategic and tactical, the latter operating within the framework imposed by the former. Whether tactical or strategic, marketing planning, requires the laying down of policies for the acquisition, use and disposal of resources.

Marketing planning as a functional area of planning activity' can only work within a corporate planning framework. The marketing planner must not lose sight of the need to achieve corporate level objectives by means of exploiting product and market combinations. Therefore, there is an underlying requirement for any organisation adopting marketing planning systems to set a clearly defined business mission as the basis from which organisational direction can develop.

DEVELOPING A MARKETING STRATEGY

A marketing strategy is a detailed explanation of how an organisation will achieve its marketing objectives. It includes two components:
- selection of a target market and
- the creation of a marketing mix that will satisfy the needs of the chosen target market.

> **MARKETING STRATEGY:** the means by which a marketing goal is to be achieved. It requires a Target Market and an appropriate Marketing Mix to reach the particular market.

TARGET MARKET SELECTION

Selecting an appropriate target market may be the most important decision a company has to make in the planning process.
1. Should the company select the wrong target market, all other marketing decisions will be a waste of time.
2. An organisation must examine whether it possesses the necessary resources and skills to create a marketing mix that will satisfy the needs of its target market.
3. Organisations must also choose their target markets carefully because of the changes taking place in the population.

CREATING THE MARKETING MIX

1. The elements of the market mix—product, distribution, promotion and price—are sometimes referred to as marketing mix variables because each can be varied or changed to accommodate the needs of the target market.
2. The decisions made in creating a marketing mix are only as good as the organisation's understanding of the target market.
3. Marketing mix decisions must also have consistency and flexibility.
4. Different elements of the marketing mix can be changed to accommodate different marketing strategies.

MARKETING TACTICS: detailed, day-to-day operational decisions essential to the overall success of marketing strategies

> ***PORTER'S GENERIC MARKETING STRATEGIES*** (1980):
>
> 1. **OVERALL COST LEADERSHIP**
>
> 2. **DIFFERENTIATION**
>   - Me-too product is not very profitable.
>   - Temporary monopoly.
>
> 3. **FOCUS/NICHE MARKETING**
>   - Usually adopted by small businesses as a means of survival.
>   - Specialised products/services.
>   - Characteristics of a niche: profitable and growing; low competition and customers' needs satisfiable.
>   - Multiple market niching.

CREATING THE MARKETING PLAN

Marketing planning is the systematic process of assessing marketing opportunities and resources, determining marketing objectives, defining marketing strategies and establishing guidelines for implementation and control of a marketing plan.

The marketing planning cycle is a circular process, with feedback used to co-ordinate and synchronise all stages of the planning cycle.

The duration of marketing plans varies.
1. Short-term plans cover a period of one year or less.
2. Medium-range plans cover two to five years.
3. Long-range plans extend beyond five years.

The extent to which marketing managers develop and use plans also varies.
1. A firm should have a plan for each marketing strategy it develops.
2. Because such plans must be changed as forces in the firm and in the environment change, marketing planning is a continuous process.
3. Although planning provides numerous benefits, some managers do not use formal marketing plans because they spend almost all their time dealing with daily problems, many of which would be eliminated by adequate planning.

COMPONENTS OF THE MARKETING PLAN

Note: there is no set outline which will work for all situations; below is a generic outline.

1. The executive summary is a brief synopsis of the entire report, including an introduction, an explanation of the major aspects of the marketing plan and a statement about the costs of implementing the plan.

2. The corporate remit This section is the foundation stone from which marketing planning commences.
- The mission, as an all-embracing statement of purpose and conduct, offers a mirror against which marketing strategy should be viewed.
- Constraints comprise the limiting resource factors within which the marketing plan should be designed and implemented.
- The corporate objectives become a source of reference for achievement, in fact, through the delivery of the marketing plan.

3. Environmental analysis provides information about the company's current situation with respect to the marketing environment; this information is obtained from both internal and external environments, usually through the firm's marketing information system and marketing research.

    a. It assesses the marketing environment - the competitive, economic, political, legal and regulatory, technological and sociocultural factors external to the firm.
    b. It examines the current situation with respect to the target market.
    c. It critically evaluates the firm's current marketing objectives and performance.

The **marketing audit** is a tool of analysis of the internal operating environment of the business and of the external market place. Both audits are produced to determine clear statements of fact. It is based upon this systematic process that clear statements of fact can then be analysed.

4. SWOT analysis. This analysis is a conversion of the marketing audit into an analysis for action. It should start with an evaluation of opportunities that are then assessed to be actionable within the planning horizons of the company. These opportunities can be classified by market segment and can be considered also against the strategic options of the Ansoff matrix.

This analysis of opportunities must then be viewed against the threats imposed by macro environmental factors such as general market trends, competitive strategy and prevailing trade cultures as well as political, economic, social and technological factors

Having assessed opportunities by threats for each market segment a set of focused opportunities can then be presented for subsequent analysis of the company's ability to achieve the ambition outlined in the focused opportunities. Therefore, opportunities and their associated threats, if any, can then be assessed against the company's capacity to exploit, i.e. their strengths and weaknesses.

A summary should then be produced upon which the plan can be based.

a. Strengths and Weaknesses (first half of the SWOT analysis)
    a. The analysis of strengths and weaknesses focuses on internal factors that give the organisation certain advantages and disadvantages in meeting the needs of its target markets.
    b. Strengths refer to competitive advantages or distinctive competencies that give the firm an advantage in meeting the needs of its target markets.
    c. Weaknesses refer to any limitations that a company might face in marketing strategy development or implementation.

DISTINCTIVE COMPETENCY: something that a firm does extremely well and which might give it a competitive advantage
---

> **SUSTAINABLE COMPETITIVE ADVANTAGE:** an advantage that is difficult to copy by competitors

   b. **Opportunities and Threats** (second half of SWOT analysis)
      a. This section focuses on factors that are external to the organisation that can greatly affect its operations.
      b. Opportunities are favourable conditions in the environment that could produce rewards for the organisation if acted upon properly.
      c. Threats refer to conditions or barriers that may prevent the firm from reaching its objectives.
      d. When internal strengths are matched to external opportunities, the organisation creates capabilities that can be used to create competitive advantages in meeting the needs of customers.
      e. Internal weaknesses should be converted into strengths and external threats into opportunities.

5. Assumptions

The audit will have produced statements of fact, but it will leave many unanswered questions arising from the SWOT analysis that has been conducted and therefore in order to move ahead assumptions must be made about the future pattern of demand, the determinants of demand and competition and the company's ability to sustain performance in accordance with market expectations throughout the marketing channel to the end user.

The process of assumption setting will lead the marketer into a contingency mode of thinking, which is a healthy outcome of this stage of the plan which should contribute to the setting of realistic objectives.

6. Time scales for the plan

Normally, companies will operate within a planning horizon of one year for the marketing plan. This period should harmonise with the financial planning period and fiscal year end of the company. Planning horizons up to three and even five years can also be viewed in perspective and become part of a rolling planning system achieved during the review periods of the marketing plan.

7. Marketing objectives

   a. A marketing objective states what is to be accomplished through marketing activities.
   b. Marketing objectives should possess certain characteristics.
      (1) They should be expressed in clear, simple terms so that all marketing personnel understand exactly what they are trying to achieve.
      (2) They should be written so that they can be measured accurately.
      (3) They should be SMART.

8. Marketing Mix strategies

Marketing strategy refers to how the firm will manage its relationships with customers so that it gains an advantage over the competition. It is at the marketing mix level that the firm will detail how it will achieve a competitive advantage in a given target market.
- To gain an advantage, the firm must do something better than the competition.
- A sustainable competitive advantage is one that cannot be copied by the competition.

Marketing mix strategies are the means by which the strategic marketing objectives are to be achieved and the planning time horizons designated.

These strategies must be compatible with the external macro environment by segment and be compatible with the competencies of the business so that they will facilitate the achievement of corporate objectives and remain consistent with the corporate mission. It is through a company's marketing mix strategies and the integration between the mix elements that a company delivers its key factors for success to the segments it serves or intends to serve.

The mix elements comprise what is simplistically known as 'the 4 Ps', i.e. Product, Price, Promotion and Place. For each of the four Ps objectives must also be set, strategies determined and policies laid down to guide the strategy

It is essential that the feasibility of these strategies is considered before they are committed to the final plan. Again the tension between ambition and ability must be assessed against an acceptable level of risk.

9. Marketing Mix tactics
Each element of the mix plan must be converted into a set of tasks for achievement. These represent discrete action programmes to be undertaken with responsibility assigned for their attainment within the time and resource limitations set.

10. Selling and sales management
The sales plan, by market segment, must be derived from the marketing plan and not be a separate document that is inconsistent with the marketing plan objectives and strategies (too often the case in many companies).

Sales quotas and targets must be set against the marketing objectives previously forecasted for market share, sales volume and sales revenue. Policies need to be laid down, sales strategies determined, sales organisation reviewed and sales management controls confirmed so that a sales budget can be produced to be added to the overall budget for the marketing plan.

11. Staffing and organisational development
Changes to head count, structure and manpower plans must be considered for the entire plan so that organisational development needs are fully anticipated before the commencement of the plan. In particular, training needs must be analysed so that the marketing plan can be accomplished within an organisation to attain programme marketing orientation. Responsibility by segment must be designated so that the company plans for the market effectively.

12. Marketing implementation
Marketing implementation is the process of putting marketing strategies into action. This section of the marketing plan answers questions about marketing activities.
(1) What specific actions will be taken?
(2) How long will these activities be performed?
(3) Who is responsible for the completion of these activities?
(4) How much will these activities cost?
Without a workable implementation plan, the success of the marketing strategy is in jeopardy.

13. Contingency plans
The planner must refer back to the assumptions that have been set. If these assumptions are not appropriate or become unfulfilled within the life of the plan, then contingency action

will become necessary.
The assumptions may be over-achieved or under-achieved and this will lead to:
- a best case scenario
- a worst case scenario

and therefore outline action needs to be proposed in advance of these events occurring (forewarned is forearmed).

Naturally, the purpose is to alert the company to the outcomes from the under or over achievement of the plan and the course of action to be taken.

14. Budgets
A detailed budget of income and expenditure with allowances for contingency is the final output of the plan. It feeds the master budget of the enterprise which in turn develops a profit and loss account for the enterprise as a whole. The budget headings should tie up with responsibility centres so that sub-budgets can be allocated back to product/market groupings once the overall budget is approved.

15. Evaluation and control
The final section of the marketing plan details how the results of the plan will be measured and evaluated. It includes the actions that can be taken to reduce the differences between planned and actual performance.

(1) Standards for assessing the actual performance need to be established.
(2) The plan needs to address the financial data used to evaluate whether the plan is working.
(3) The firm can use a number of monitoring procedures to pinpoint causes for any discrepancies.

The marketing objectives as laid down in the plan and the marketing mix objectives which have been set represent standards of performance. The review of the plan is primarily set against these objectives and then subsequently for the strategies which achieved, or did not achieve, the objectives. In particular, it is a review of the performance of the marketing team. Accountability and responsibility are measured against performance in the market place.

Monthly, quarterly, half-yearly and annual reviews are essential so that forecasted performance can be compared with actual achievement. The budgetary control system, sales information system and MkIS have a vital role to play.

USING THE MARKETING PLAN
1. The creation and implementation of a complete marketing plan will allow the organisation to achieve not only its marketing objectives, but also its business-unit and corporate objectives.
2. The marketing plan is only as good as the information it contains and the effort and creativity that went into its development.
3. Every marketing plan is and should be unique to the organisation for which it was created.
4. The marketing plan should be flexible enough so that it can be adjusted on a daily basis.

Professionalism in marketing needs a well conceived planning system - yet too many companies remain sales oriented and manage by crisis through periods of sales target reviews alone. Such a system demands support from the chief executive officer and top management, needs a plan for planning, needs supportive line management, a compliant corporate culture and a management team who are motivated and indeed incentivised into the use of the system as an on-going planning tool

SOME ISSUES ASSOCIATED WITH PLANNING

SEGMENTING, TARGETING & POSITIONING (STP)

1. MARKET SEGMENTATION: dividing a market into distinct groups of buyers with different needs, characteristics or behaviour who might require separate products or marketing mixes

> **MARKET SEGMENT:** a group of consumers who respond in a similar way to a given set of marketing stimuli

2. MARKET TARGETING: the process of evaluating each market segment's attractiveness and selecting one or more segments to enter

3. MARKET POSITIONING
This involves:
- arranging for a product to occupy a clear, distinctive and desirable place in the minds of target consumers
- formulating competitive positioning for a product and a detailed marketing mix

MARKETING MANAGEMENT

> TOPIC: MARKETING RESEARCH
> LECTURE: 5

MARKETING INFORMATION SYSTEMS & MARKETING RESEARCH

In carrying out their marketing responsibilities, marketing managers need a great deal of information. In order to implement the marketing concept they require information about the characteristic, needs, wants and desires of their target markets. Remember that no army goes into battle without "intelligence".

THE ROLE OF MARKETING RESEARCH IN DECISION MAKING
The 3 Functional Roles of Marketing Research:
1. Descriptive Function - the gathering and presentation of statements of fact.
2. Diagnostic Function - The explanation of data.
3. Predictive Function - Specification of how to use the descriptive and diagnostic research to predict the result of a planned marketing decision.

The Importance of Marketing Research to management is highlighted by its three basic uses: (represents applied research)
1. Improving the quality of decision making
2. Finding out what went wrong
3. Understanding the marketplace

Despite the growing supply of information, managers often lack enough information of the right kind or have too much of the wrong kind. To overcome these problems, many companies are taking steps to improve their marketing information systems. The more information the better the decisions, the greater the competitive advantage. Knowing the customer, the market and the competition better than anyone else is the key to success.

A Marketing information System (MkIS) is a planned, orderly, continuous collection, analysis and presentation of information to marketing managers for marketing decisions.

Marketing Research (MR), on the other hand, is a systematic gathering, recording and analysing of information about specific issues related to marketing.

MkIS differs from marketing research in that it is wider in scope and involves the ongoing collection and analysis of marketing data. MR is a sub-system of a MkIS. A MkIS is pro-active, while marketing research is reactive.

A well-designed marketing information system first assesses information needs. The MkIS next develops information and helps managers to use it more effectively. The marketing information system distributes information gathered from
- Internal Sources
- Marketing Intelligence
- Marketing Research
- Decision Support Systems

to the right managers at the right time.

Marketing research involves collecting information relevant to a specific marketing problem facing the company. MR is used for any aspect of marketing that requires information for decision making. It can help:
- Identify market (consumer) characteristics
- Determine attitudes, behaviour
- Determine demographics
- Estimate market potential
- Market share analysis
- Product research
- Short range forecasting

Both a MkIS and MR are used to reduce business risk, exploit opportunities and minimise new product failures. In the 1990s the failure rate of new products is in excess of 80%.

THE MARKETING INFORMATION SYSTEM
THE IMPORTANCE OF INFORMATION TO THE MARKETING MANAGER

- **The Marketing Environment** Companies compete in an environment of Social, Legal, Cultural, Technological, Natural and Competitive dimensions. Information on each aspect of the environment is crucial to effective market planning.
- **Customer Needs and Wants** If environmental forces cause the company to seek information in a larger context, customer needs and wants focuses the attention on the target market. Constant timely information of needs and wants and how they change must be part of any marketing effort.
- **Competitors** The actions of competitors cannot go unnoticed by the company.
- **Strategic Decision Making** Strategy formulation depends upon accurate and timely information.

COMPONENTS OF THE MkIS

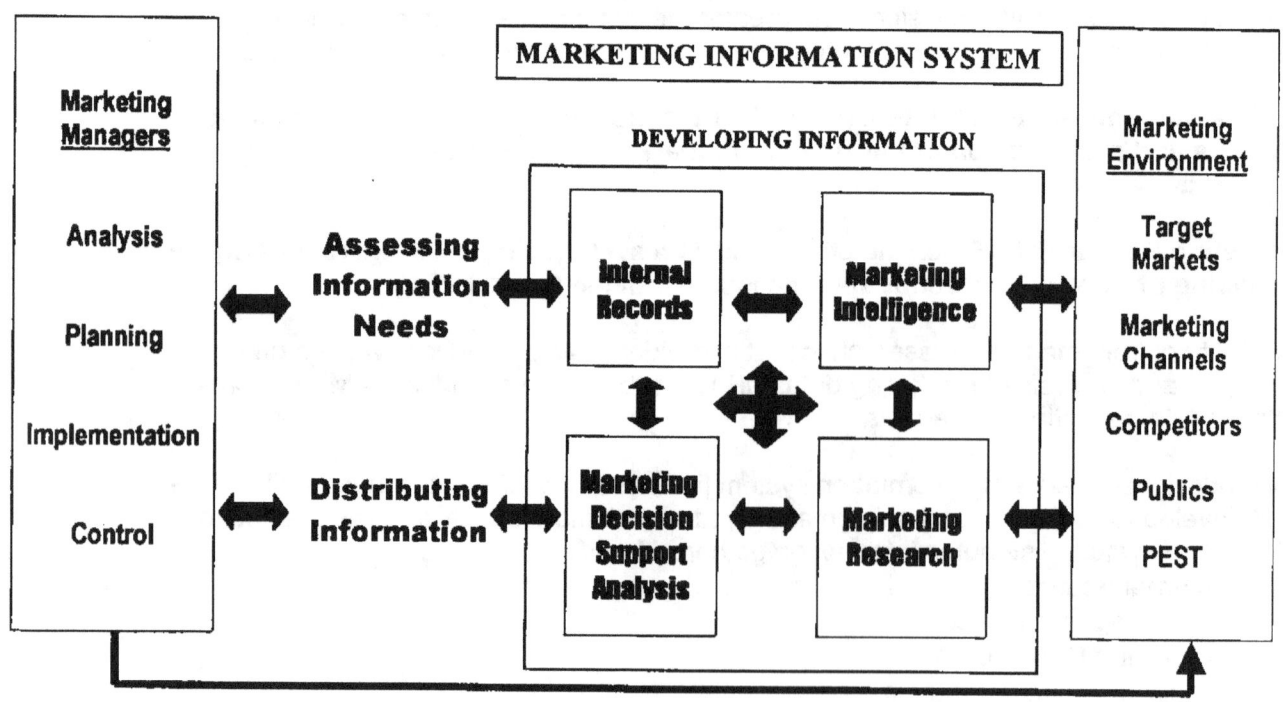

Marketing Decisions and Communications

ASSESSING INFORMATION NEEDS involves knowing what is needed or likely to be needed is a key feature of the MkIS. This underscores the importance of information.

DEVELOPING INFORMATION

1. Internal Records provide a wealth of information which is essentially raw data for decision making. An effective MkIS organises and summarises balance sheets, orders, schedules, shipments and inventories into trends that can be linked to management decisions on marketing mix changes.

2. Marketing Intelligence provides the everyday information about environmental variables that managers need as they implement and adjust marketing plans. Sources for intelligence may vary according to needs but may include both internal and external sources.

3. Marketing Research links the consumer, customer and public to the marketer through an exchange of information. Research is often project oriented:
- **Exploratory studies** Searching for questions or problems. Focus groups used to identify issues for later exploration in surveys
- **Descriptive Studies** e.g. Identify what "is" the Profile of customers
- **Causal Studies** e.g. How does the amount of advertising affect sales
  Sales=f(Advertising)

4. Marketing Decision Support Analysis (DSS)
Computer software has been available to marketing managers for some time. Computer software has been available to marketing managers for some time. Decision Support Systems (DSS) can function is many ways. They can:
- organise information for decision situation
- interact with decision makers
- expand the decision makers' horizons
- present information for decision makers' understanding
- add structure to decisions
- use multiple-criteria decision-making models

INFORMATION ANALYSIS
requires that the MkIS director anticipate how the information is to be used.
If MkIS generates reports from raw data with plenty of lead-time, analysis issues are more a MkIS department matter. But if users from all business functions use the MkIS on-line for short deadline decisions, then the analytical tools each area needs must be available on demand.

DISTRIBUTING INFORMATION
Distributing information requires integrating marketing manager's need for certain types and forms of information with the MkIS'
- hardware
- software and

personnel design.

THE MARKETING RESEARCH PROCESS

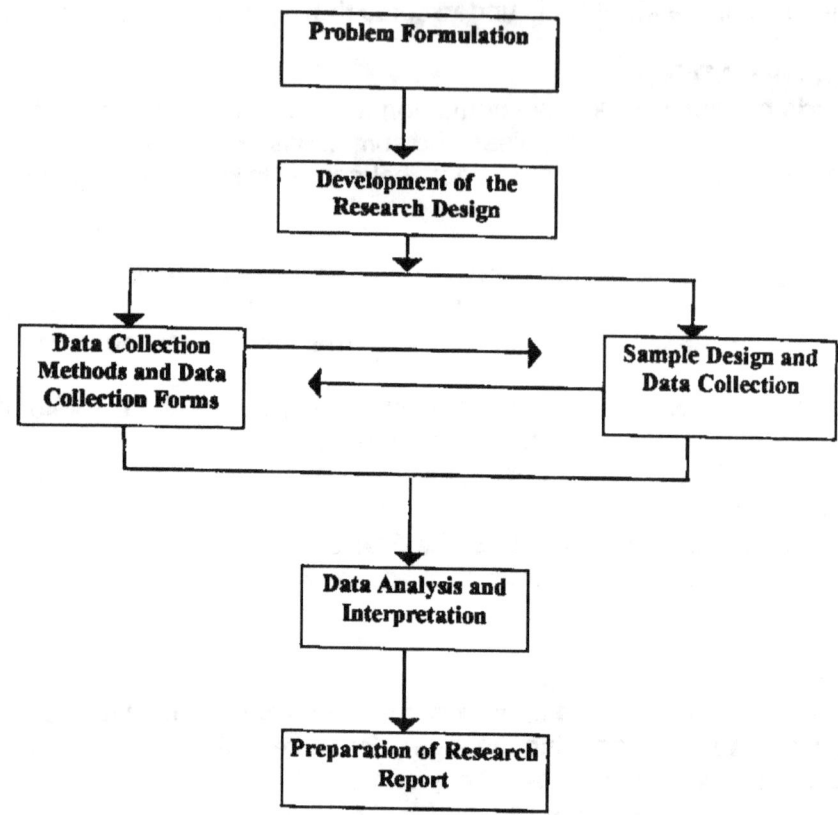

This is a general approach to conducting marketing research and is applicable to:
- Organisations of all types
- Various and sundry marketing issues

1. DEFINING THE PROBLEM
Before researchers can provide managers with information, they must know what kind of problem the manager wishes to solve. Symptoms are often identified as problems something which is incorrect.

To successfully complete this first step may require exploratory research to clearly define issue. Correct problem definition is key to a successful undertaking. One must precisely formulate and define the opportunity, issue or problem.

Informational Problems
1. Lack information, Outdated information
Examples
- We don't have a profile of our customers so we don't know who to target our ads to or what benefits to stress to those customers.
- Where should we locate our new retail store?
- Did our ads work?

2. Performance problems
Examples   Sales are below expectations, why?
Losing market share, to whom and for what reasons?

2. DEVELOPING THE RESEARCH PLAN
The framework or plan for a study that guides the collection and analysis of data, it includes:
- Who collects the data?
- What should be collected?
- Who or what should be studied
- What technique of data collection should be used?
- How much will the study cost?
- How will data be collected (personnel)?
- How long will data collection take?

It involves all of the following
- **Determining Specific Information Needs.** What type of information is necessary to research this defined issue and where can one secure such information.
- **Gathering Secondary Information.** There are secondary sources, which may be internal or external of the firm, but offer information previously gathered for some other reason than the current problem. It should be checked first. It is low in cost and readily available. However, secondary information was not gathered for this problem and therefore perhaps is not quite relevant. Its credibility is questionable if from an outside source. It may also be outdated.
- **Planning Primary Data Collection Research Approaches.** This is information collected for the specific problem. It should be used only if necessary. It is more expensive and takes time to collect. But it is specific to the needs of the study and the researcher knows the source and collection method. There are 4 common approaches for gathering primary data:

    Observations ("watch and record" Record overt behaviour, note physical conditions and events.) are linked to actual behaviours but may not help in understanding why people act as they do.
    e.g. "How long does a McDonald's customer have to wait in line". Can be combined with interviews, i.e. get demographic variables. To avoid bias must avoid being seen.
    (Mechanical observation devices - cameras, eye movement recorders, galvanometers, scanner technology)

    Surveys (questionnaires by telephone, mail or person to person) can help describe reasons for people's behaviour and provide the research with flexibility. Focus groups are very popular. They seek details from a small number of informed consumers.
    Design data collection forms - Questionnaire Design

    Experimental methods help identify cause and effect relationships - independent and dependent variables are identified & assessed to determine how one affects other

    Simulation – (model building of variables) The process by which a model displays the characteristics and behaviour of the real world.

Data Sources:
a. Primary Data (Field Research)
- Quantitative Data - Numerical data: Samples, Surveys, Enumeration
- Qualitative Data - Feelings, emotions, opinions: Focus groups, surveys, observations

Advantages of Primary data
- Problem-oriented
- More accurate and valid information
- Methodology is controlled and known
- Available to firm and secret from competitors
- Only way to fill a gap.

Disadvantages of Primary data
- Time consuming
- Costly to obtain
- Some information cannot be collected

b. Secondary Data (Desk Research)
- Published Sources – Libraries, Government Statistics, Trade Press
- Commercially Available
- On-line e.g. the Internet

Advantages of secondary data
- Saves time
- Is cheaper to obtain
- Increases research efficiency
- Can be used as a comparative tool
- Obtain information that cannot be obtained through primary research
- Multiple sources available
- Independent therefore credible.

Disadvantages of secondary data
- Carries over primary flaws in earlier data
- May not be appropriate
- Data may not be in the form or detail required
- Data may be old
- Methodology maybe unknown, reliability may be unproven

In any case: Both are needed!

Contact Methods
- mail
- telephone
- personal.

Sampling Plans
address the
- **who** (sampling unit)
- **how many** (sample size), and
- **how to choose**

decisions of drawing a sample (probability or nonprobability).

Sampling - To select representative units from a total population.
A population "universe" consists of all elements, units or individuals that are of interest to researchers for a specific study i.e. all registered voters for an election.

Sampling procedures are used in studying the likelihood of events based on assumptions about the future.
   Random sampling - equal chance for each member of the population
   Stratified sampling - population divided into groups i.e. a common characteristic, random sample each group
   Area sampling - as above using areas
   Quota sampling, judgmental - sampling error cannot be measured statistically, mainly used in exploratory studies to develop a hypothesis, non-probabilistic.

Research Instruments
may include mechanical or electronic devices although the survey questionnaire is the most common instrument.

3. COLLECTING INFORMATION
Before collecting the information, the Research Plan must be presented the manager or client for approval. Following approval the plan is then implemented.

In implementing the plan care must be taken that all personnel involved in collecting and analysing data understand clearly the purpose of the research and are adequately trained and experienced to complete it professionally.

Methods of collecting information include
- surveys and
- experiments

using
- mail questionnaires
- telephone interviewing and
- personal interviewing.

4. INTERPRETING THE FINDINGS
Interpreting research findings may involve statistical analyses or not but these tools of analysis should not be confused with the action-oriented information needed by marketing managers.

5. REPORTING THE FINDINGS
The researchers' findings are presented to the parties involved. The findings should be relevant to the problem at hand and aid management decision-making.

International Marketing Research
needs to take into consideration cultural and legal differences for each market.

Public Policy and Ethics in Marketing Research
issues include intrusions on consumer privacy and MkIS use of research findings.

MARKETING MANAGEMENT

> **TOPIC: CONSUMER BUYING BEHAVIOUR**
> **LECTURE: 6**

CONSUMER BUYING BEHAVIOUR

Definition: Buying Behaviour is the decision processes and acts of people involved in buying and using products.

Consumer buying behaviour refers to the buying behaviour of final consumers - individuals and households who buy goods and services for personal consumption. All of these final consumers make up the consumer market.

In earlier times, marketers could understand consumers well through the daily experience of selling to them. But as firms and markets have grown in size, many marketing decision-makers have lost direct contact with their customers and must now turn to consumer research. They now spend more money than ever to study consumers, trying to learn more about consumer behaviour. Marketers need to understand:

- Who buys the organisation's products and services
- What do they buy
- Why consumers make the purchases that they make
- How do they buy
- When, Where, How often,
- What factors influence consumer purchases
- The changing factors in our society

The central question for marketers is: How do consumers respond to various marketing stimuli the organisation might use? The company that really understands how consumers will respond to different product features, prices and advertising appeals has a great advantage over its competitors. Therefore, a firm needs to analyse buying behaviour because:

- Buyers' reactions to a firm's marketing strategy have a great impact on the firm's success.
- The marketing concept stresses that a firm should create a Marketing Mix that satisfies (gives utility to) customers, therefore what, where, when and how consumers buy needs to be analysed.
- Marketers can predict better how consumers will respond to marketing strategies.

The model of consumer behaviour shows that marketing and other stimuli enter the consumer's **'black box'** and produce certain responses. Marketers must try to understand what is in the buyer's black box.

The external factors which may affect a potential buyer consist of the marketing mix offered by a supplier plus various environmental issues such as the economic situation, technological developments, the media, political and legal influences, cultural differences and competitor marketing mixes.

What is the buyer's 'Black Box'?

A buyer's 'black box' is really a combination of internal factors, consisting of the stages through which an individual passes on the way to a purchase decision, plus the various personal characteristics any individual will possess. These will be a combination of cultural influences; social context, such as social groups or family values; psychological make-up; and personal circumstances. Personal circumstances will include socio-economic position, life-cycle stage, life style etc. Psychological profiles are more complicated and will involve factors such as an individual's motivation; perception; values and attitudes.

Marketing stimuli consist of the four Ps (marketing mix variables). Other stimuli include significant forces and events in the buyer's environment: economic, technological, political and cultural. All these stimuli enter the buyer's black box where they are turned into a set of observable buyer responses.

The marketer wants to understand how the stimuli are changed into responses inside the consumer's black box, which has two parts.
- the buyers characteristics influence how he or she perceives and reacts to the stimuli
- the buyer's decision process itself affects the buyer's behaviour.

INFLUENCES ON CONSUMER PURCHASE DECISION PROCESS

Marketing Mix
Product
Price
Place
Promotion

Psychological Influences
- Motivation and personality
- Perception
- Learning
- Attitudes

Consumer Decision Process
- Problem recognition
- Information Search
- Alternative Evaluation
- Purchase Decision
- Postpurchase Behaviour

Socio-Cultural Influences
- Personal Influences
- Social Class
- Reference Groups
- Culture
- Family

Situation Factors
- Purchase Task
- Temporal Effects
- Social Surroundings
- Antecedent states
- Physical conditions

FACTORS THAT INFLUENCE CONSUMER BEHAVIOUR

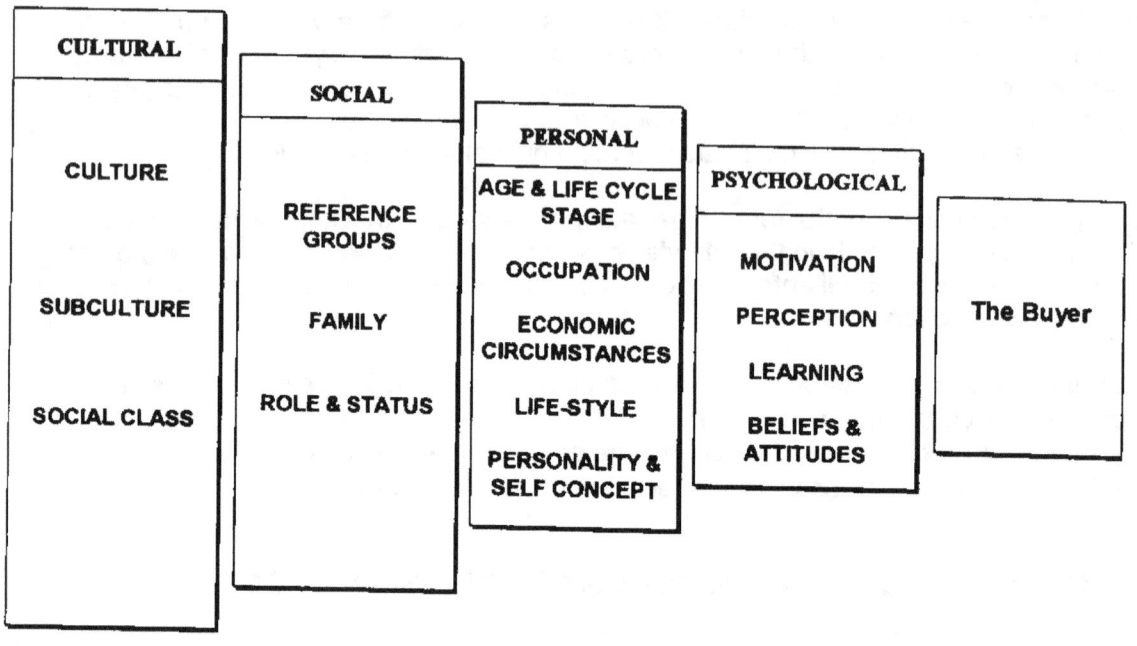

1. CULTURAL FACTORS.
Cultural factors exert the broadest and deepest influence on consumer behaviour. The marketer needs to understand the role played by the buyer's culture, subculture and social class.

a. Culture
Culture (the values, beliefs, preferences and tastes handed down from one generation to another) is the most basic cause of a person's wants and behaviour. Human behaviour is largely learned. Growing up in a society, a child learns basic values, perceptions, wants and behaviours from the family and other important institutions. Core values are stable within a cultural group. Marketers are always trying to spot cultural shifts in order to imagine new products that might be wanted.

Cultural groups are not homogeneous and may be broken down into subcultures

b. Subculture.
Each culture contains smaller subcultures or groups of people with shared value systems based on common life experiences and situations. Subcultures include nationalities, religions, racial groups, and geographic regions.

c. Social Class.
Almost every society has some form of social class structure. Social classes are society's relatively permanent and ordered divisions whose members share similar values, interests and behaviours.

> **_Seven Social Classes_**
> 1. Upper-upper 1% - inherit wealth, well known families
> 2. Lower-Upper 2% - achieve success through exceptional ability - need status symbols
> 3. Upper-Middles 12% - professionals
> 4. Middle 32% - keep up with the trends
> 5. Working 38%
> 6. Upper lowers 9%
> 7. Lower-lowers 7%

2. SOCIAL FACTORS

A consumer's behaviour is also influences by social factors, such as the consumer's small groups, family, and social roles and status. Because these social factors can strongly affect consumer responses, companies must take them into account when designing their marketing strategies.

a. Reference Groups

A person's behaviour is influenced by many small that serve as direct or indirect points of comparison or reference in forming a person's attitudes or behaviour
- **Membership Groups** - Groups which have a direct influence and to which a person belongs
- **Primary Groups** - friends, family, co-workers
- **Secondary Groups** - religious, professional
- **Aspirational Groups** – groups to which the individual aspires to belong
- **Dissociative Groups** - the sets of people which the consumer wishes to avoid

b. Family.

Family members can strongly influence buyer behaviour. We can distinguish between two families in the buyer's life.
- *The family of orientation* - The buyer's parents make up the family of orientation. Parents provide a person with orientation towards religion, politics and economics and a sense of personal ambition, self-worth and love. Even if the buyer no longer interacts very much with parents, they can still significantly influence the buyer's behaviour.
- *The family of procreation* - the buyer's spouse and children - has a more direct influence on everyday buying behaviour.

c. Consumers' buying roles.

Group members can influence purchases in many ways.
- *Initiator (Starter)* - The person who first suggests or thinks of the idea of buying a particular product or service.
- *Influencer* - A person whose view or advice influences the buying decision, perhaps a friend or a salesperson.
- *Decider* - The person who ultimately makes a buying decision or any part of it - whether to buy, what to buy, how to buy or where to buy.
- *Purchaser* - The person who makes an actual purchase.
- *End-User* - The person who consumes or uses a product or service.
- *Financier* – The person who pays for the purchase

3. PERSONAL FACTORS
A person's decisions also are influenced by personal characteristics such as the

a. Age and Life-Cycle Stage - People change the goods and services they buy over their lifetimes as their needs and tastes change

b. Occupation - A person's occupation affects the goods and services bought. Marketers try to identify the occupational groups that have above-average interest in their products and services.

c. Income

d. Lifestyle - Activities, interests, opinions (AIO) Lifestyle is a person's pattern of living as expressed in his or her activities, interests and opinions

e. Personality and Self-Concept - Personality refers to the unique psychological characteristics that lead to relatively consistent and lasting responses to one's own environment. Personality is usually described in terms of traits such as self-confidence, dominance, sociability, defensiveness, adaptability, and aggressiveness. Many marketers use a concept related to personality - a person's self-concept. The basic self-concept premise is that people's possessions contribute to and reflect their identities: that is, 'we are what we have'.

4. PSYCHOLOGICAL FACTORS.
A person's buying choices are further influenced by four important psychological factors: motivation, perception, learning, and beliefs and attitudes.

a. Motivation
A person has many needs at any given time. Some are biological, arising from states of tension such as hunger, thirst or discomfort. Others are psychological, arising from the need for recognition, esteem or belonging. Most of these needs will not be strong enough to motivate the person to act at a given point in time. A need becomes a motive when it is aroused to a sufficient level of intensity. A motive is a need that is sufficiently pressing to direct the person to seek satisfaction.

Maslow's theory of motivation illustrates human needs arranged in a hierarchy, from the most pressing to the least pressing. In order of importance they are:
- **Physiological needs** - Thirst, Hunger, Sleep, Exercise
- **Security Needs** - Safety
- **Social Needs** - Belong to groups
- **Esteem Needs** - Be recognised in the group
- **Self Actualisation Needs** - The Highest order of needs - To achieve one's potential

b. Perception - How people interpret information
A motivated person is ready to act. How the person acts is influenced by his or her perception of the situation. Two people with the same motivation and in the same situation may act quite differently because they perceive the situation differently. Why do people perceive the same situation differently? All of us learn by the flow of information through our five senses: sight, hearing, smell, touch and taste. However, each of us receives, organises and interprets this sensory information in an individual way.

Thus, perception is the process by which people select, organise and interpret information to form a meaningful picture of the world and is influenced by:

- Selective attention which may depend on
    - Current need for a product
    - Expectation
    - Large deviations from current views held
- Selective distortion
- Selective retention
- Subliminal perception

c. **Learning**- changes in behaviour from experience
When people act, they learn. Learning describes changes in an individual's behaviour arising from experience. Learning occurs through the interplay of drives, stimuli, cues, responses and reinforcement.

The practical significance of learning theory for marketers is that they can build up demand for a product by associating it with motivating cues and providing positive reinforcement.

d. **Beliefs and Attitudes.**
Through doing and learning, people acquire their beliefs and attitudes.
- A belief is a descriptive thought that a person has about something.
- An attitude describes a person's relatively consistent and enduring favourable/unfavourable evaluations based on:
    - Cognitive evaluations
    - Emotional feelings and
    - Action tendencies towards an object or idea e.g. purchase

How to change attitudes
- **Change Beliefs** - e.g. McDonald's Burger is low in cholesterol
- **Change Importance** - e.g. Low calories or taste
- **Add New Attributes** - e.g. Air bags for passenger and driver
- **Change Behaviour** – e.g. by law as in the case of seat belts

TYPES OF CONSUMER BUYING BEHAVIOUR.
Buying behaviour is the decision processes and acts of people involved in buying and using products. Consumer buying behaviour is the buying behaviour of persons who purchase products for personal or household use and not for business purposes. A firm's success and the satisfaction of its customers are directly related to marketers' understanding of buying behaviour.

Buying Behaviour depends on
- Degree of Involvement - High or low
- Differences between brands - large or small

Differences between Brands	HIGH INVOLVEMENT	LOW INVOLVEMENT
LARGE	Complex Buying Behaviour	Variety Seeking Behaviour
SMALL	Dissonance Reducing Behaviour	Habitual Buying Behaviour

CONSUMER BUYING BEHAVIOUR AND DECISION MAKING

There are four major types of consumer buying behaviour in terms of the decision making required on the part of the consumer:

1. Routine Response Behaviour.
Involves very little search and decision effort. Used for products that are low prices and bought frequently and quickly.

2. Limited Decision-Making.
Used for products purchased occasionally and/or to acquire information about unfamiliar brands in a familiar product category. Requires a moderate amount of time.

3. Extensive Decision-Making.
Buyers use many criteria for evaluating brands and spend more time seeking alternative products and searching for information about the products. Extensive decisions are made by consumers buying expensive products such as cars, houses etc. and infrequently purchased less expensive items.

4. Impulse Buying.
Impulse buying involves no conscious planning, but a powerful, persistent urge to buy something immediately.

THE 5 STAGES OF THE CONSUMER BUYING PROCESS

Consumer decision making is essentially a problem-solving process. The more marketers know about this process, the greater their ability to influence the process with attractive products and marketing programs. It should be noted that:
- The actual act of purchase is only one stage in the process.
- Not all decision process, once initiated, lead to an ultimate purchase.
- The individual may terminate the process at any stage.
- Not all consumer decisions include all five stages but they are determined by the degree of complexity of the purchase decision.

FLOWCHART OF THE PURCHASE DECISION PROCESS

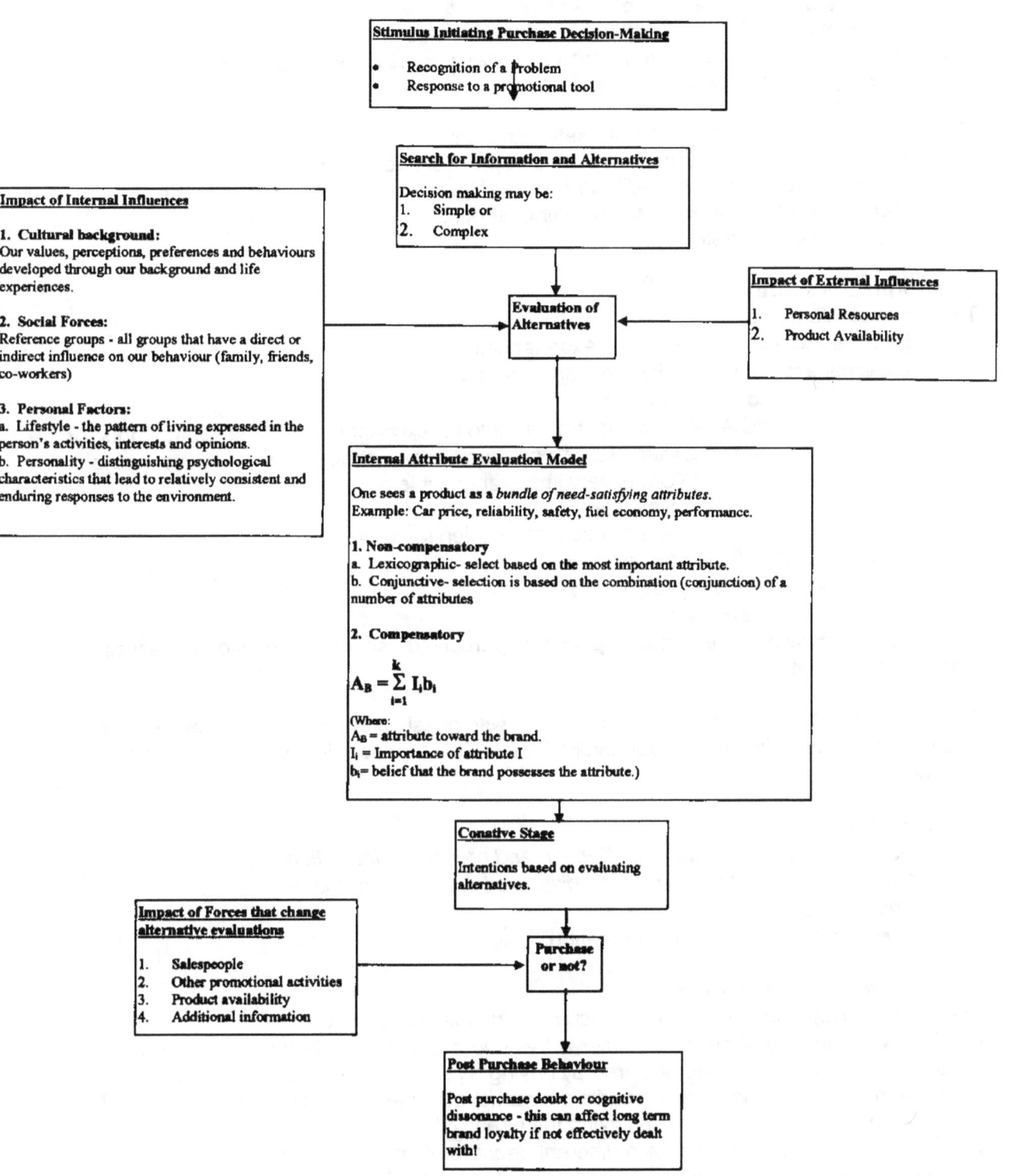

THE CONSUMER BUYING DECISION PROCESS (*For complex decisions*).

1. Problem Recognition (Awareness of Need)
This is the difference between the desired state and the actual condition.
    E.g. **Hunger → Food.** Hunger stimulates the need to eat.
Sometimes a consumer may have a problem or need but is unaware of it and the speed of problem recognition can be slow or rapid.

The need can be stimulated by the marketer through:
- showing inadequacy of current state and product information
  i.e. *do you know you are deficient?* e.g. a Nike advertisement stimulates the recognition of the need for a new pair of shoes.
- showing desired state

2. Information search
Two types of information search:
- **Internal search:** memory, past experiences.
- **External search** if more information is needed.
  - Friends and relatives
    WOM (word of mouth) refers to an exchange of comments, thoughts, or ideas between two or more consumers, none of whom is a marketing source. WOM is very important as it is:
    - Believable
    - Often comes from opinion leaders
  - Marketer dominated sources
  - comparison shopping
  - public sources etc.

How much the consumer searches depends on perceived risk. Also, repetition increases learning of information.

A successful information search leaves a buyer with possible alternatives, **the evoked set**. E.g. Hungry, want to go out and eat, evoked set is Chinese food, Indian food, McDonald's, KFC etc

Marketing action:
- *Use packaging that captures attention and provides information*
- *Make sure product is prominently displayed and easily available*
- *Price for value*
- *Use promotion to provide information*

3. Evaluation of Alternatives
Certain basic concepts help explain consumer evaluation processes.
- First, we assume that each consumer is trying to satisfy some need and is looking for certain benefits that can be acquired by buying a product or service. Further, each consumer sees a product as a bundle of product attributes with varying capacities for delivering these benefits and satisfying the need.
- Second, the consumer will attach different degrees of importance to each attribute.
- Third, the consumer is likely to develop a set of brand beliefs about where each brand stands on each attribute.

At this stage consumers establish a set of criteria for comparing products and evaluation e.g.
- performance
- price
- reliability
- dealer reputation
- product features.

Consumers then rate and eventually rank the choices in the selected group of alternatives. If not satisfied with choice the consumer may return to the search phase. Information from different sources may be treated differently.

Marketing action:
- *Make sure our brand does well on important attributes*
- *Modify brand if necessary to do well on important attributes*
- *Communicate performance on important attributes*

4. Purchase decision

The consumer selects the product and the seller. Choosing a buying alternative may include product, package, store, purchasing method terms of sale etc. This can be Influenced through point-of-purchase (POP) and the sales force.

Marketing action:
- *Create pleasing store atmosphere*
- *Train salespeople*
- *Make financing easy*

5. Post-purchase evaluation

Did the product and purchase experience meet or exceed expectations? Outcome of the purchase may be Satisfaction or Dissatisfaction.

The consumer may experience **Cognitive Dissonance** i.e. Doubt whether the right decision was made. This can be reduced by warranties, after sales communication, reinforcement (pat-on-the-back) adverting etc. offered by the firm

Marketing action:
- *Provide 080 numbers*
- *Offer liberal return/refund policies*
- *Train staff to handle complaints*
- *Record and implement, if possible, customer suggestions*
- *Offer upgrades*

MARKETING MANAGEMENT

| TOPIC: BUSINESS BUYER BEHAVIOUR |
| LECTURE: 7 |

BUSINESS MARKETS AND BUSINESS BUYER BEHAVIOUR

BUSINESS MARKETS

The business market consists of all the organisations that buy goods and services to use in the production of other products and services that are sold rented or supplied to others.

It also includes retailing and wholesaling firms that acquire goods for the purpose of reselling or renting them to others at a profit. The organisational buying process is the decision-making process by which business buyers establish the need for purchased products and services, and identify, evaluate and choose among alternative brands and suppliers. Companies that sell to other business organisations must do their best to understand business markets and business buyer behaviour.

There are three major types of business markets:
- the industrial market,
- the reseller market
- the government market.

The business market is huge: most businesses just sell to other businesses and sales to businesses far outstrip those to consumers. The reason for this is the number of times that a part of a consumer product is bought, processed and resold before reaching the final consumer.

In many ways, business markets are like consumer markets, but in other ways they are much different. Business markets usually have fewer but larger buyers who are more geographically concentrated. Business demand is derived, largely inelastic and more fluctuating. More buyers are usually involved in the Business buying decision and business buyers are better trained and more professional than consumer buyers are. Business purchasing decisions are more complex and the buying process is more formal.

CHARACTERISTICS OF BUSINESS MARKETS

Business markets are similar to consumer markets. Both involve people who assume buying roles and make purchase decisions to satisfy needs. However, business markets differ in many ways from consumer markets. The main differences are in market structure and demand, the nature of the buying unit and the types of decisions and the decision process involved.

1. Market Structure and Demand

Business markets have relatively few buyers, are geographically concentrated, are characterised by derived demand and are more inelastic than consumer markets.

2. *The Nature of the Buying Unit*
The decision to buy follows a rational decision making process and may require a Decision-Making Unit (DMU) including any of the following: *Starter, Specifier, Purchaser, Advocate, Decider, End-User, Financier, Gatekeeper.*
- Business markets have buyers who are more likely to be technical or well-qualified people and use more professional purchasing procedures.
- Buyers may have considerable buying power and are of high management status.

3. *Types of Decisions and the Decision Process*
Business buying is a more complex and formal process than consumer buying. Purchases may be irregular or infrequent.

4. *Other Characteristics*
Business markets are also characterised by Direct Purchasing from producers, Reciprocity in selecting suppliers who also buy from them, Leasing, rather than buying equipment.

BUYING PATTERNS OF INDUSTRIAL CUSTOMERS

1. Length of negotiation period
Usually much longer because;
    a. Several executives are involved
    b. The sale involves a large amount of money
    c. Considerable discussion is involved in establishing specifications
    d. Bids are often involved requiring careful estimates

2. Frequency of purchase varies considerably
e.g.   a. Installations every 15 years
        b. Office supplies every month
        c. Annual contracts for services

3. Size of order is usually large

4. Direct purchase
Direct selling from the manufacturer to the industrial customer is quite common.

5. Multiple influences on purchase
The purchase decision is influenced by a number of different people who may:
- initiate purchase project
- determine product specifications
- select the supplier

6. Reciprocal trading
"I will buy from you if you buy from me"

7. Demand for product servicing
The complexities of technological products mean that a great deal of service is required. The provision of service may be more important than price.

BUSINESS BUYER BEHAVIOR

A. MAJOR TYPES OF BUYING SITUATIONS
1. **Straight Rebuy** Here the buyer reorders something without any modifications.
2. **Modified Rebuy** In this situation, the buyer seeks a change in specifications, prices, terms or suppliers.
3. **New Task** Here the company is buying the product for the first time and faces the greater costs and risks.

B. SYSTEMS BUYING AND SELLING
Under systems buying, the buyer seeks a packaged solution to a problem from a single seller. The seller offers a set of interlocking products and the co-ordination, implementation and control procedures for operating them.

C. PARTICIPANTS IN THE BUSINESS BUYING PROCESS
1. **Starter** - somebody who identifies the need for a purchase
2. **Specifiers** – draw up the specifications, minimum requirements etc.
3. **Users** - are members of the organisation who will use the product.
4. **Influencers** - are people who affect the buying decision.
5. **Purchasers** - are those with the formal authority to select suppliers and to arrange terms of purchase.
6. **Deciders** - have the formal or informal power to select or approve the final suppliers.
7. **Financier** – the provider of the necessary finance for the purchase
8. **Gatekeepers** - are those who control the flow of information to others.

D. MAJOR INFLUENCES ON BUSINESS BUYERS

1. Environmental Factors - The business buyer operates in a competitive environment consisting of two categories. As with consumer markets:
- Marketing stimuli consist of the product, place, price and promotion
- Other stimuli consist of the forces in the economic, technological, political, cultural and competitive environments. Business Buyers are heavily influenced by the economic environment especially the level of primary demand, economic outlook and the cost of money.

2. Organisational Factors - The buying organisation is influenced by the overall organisation - its corporate culture and values, traditions, objectives, policies, and procedures and regulations. The buying centre and the buying decision process are also part of organisational influences.

3. Interpersonal Factors - centre on group dynamics and the interplay of personalities and organisational roles.

4. Individual Factors - such as a person's age, status, education, professional speciality and overall personality and attitudes affect how they participate in organisational buying decisions.

E. BUSINESS BUYING DECISION PROCESS

1. Problem Recognition - can result from internal or external stimuli. They may emerge from an identified shortage or ideas for improvements recognised by buyers.

2. General Need Description - describes the overall characteristics and quantities of the needed item.

3. Product Specification - requires that a developmental team must translate general needs into product specifications. An engineering value analysis team may look at alternative designs to reduce production costs.

4. Supplier Search - conducts a search for the best vendors for the product specifications.

5. Proposal Solicitation - invites qualified suppliers to submit proposals covering the terms of supply and support.

6. Supplier Selection - selects suppliers based upon a combination of technical competence and service record and reputation.

7. Order-Routine Specification - specifies the details of the supplier contract listing technical specifications, delivery terms, policies for return and warranties and quantities needed.

8. Performance Review - will review how the supplier contract is working for the company and may continue, amend or drop the seller.

INSTITUTIONAL AND GOVERNMENT MARKETS

- **A. Institutional Markets** (establishments which have people under their care i.e. hospitals, schools, prisons)
  Institutional markets are characterised by low budgets and captive patrons.

- **B. Government Markets**
  Governments engage in centralised buying. Governments are also carefully watched by outside publics and subject to public review. Non-economic criteria also influence government buying decisions. Governments require suppliers to submit bids.

MARKETING MANAGEMENT

TOPIC: SEGMENTATION, TARGETING & POSITIONING
LECTURE: 8

MARKET SEGMENTATION, TARGETING AND POSITIONING.

Sellers can take three approaches to a market:
- **Mass Marketing** is the decision to mass-produce, mass-distribute and mass promote one product and attempt to attract all kinds of buyers.
- **Product-Variety Marketing** is the decision to produce two or more market offers differentiated in style, features, quality or sizes, designed to offer variety to the market and to set the seller's products apart from competitors' products.
- **Target Marketing** is the decision to identify the different groups that make up a market and to develop products and marketing mixes for selected target markets. Sellers are moving away from mass marketing and product differentiation toward target marketing.

The key steps in target marketing are market **Segmentation**, market **Targeting** and market **Positioning** (**STP**).

MARKET SEGMENTATION

Market segmentation is the process of dividing a market into distinct groups of buyers exhibiting homogeneous characteristics who might require separate products or marketing mixes.

SEGMENTING A MARKET

Buyers are divided into classes who differ in their product needs or buying responses and who are often identified by varied combinations of factors, such as age and income.

BASES FOR SEGMENTING CONSUMER MARKETS

1. Geographic Segmentation - divides the market into different geographic units based upon physical proximity.

2. Demographic Segmentation - consists of dividing the market into groups based upon variables such as sex, age, family size, family life cycle, income, education, occupation, religious affiliation or nationality.

3. Psychographic Segmentation - divides the market into groups based upon variables such as sex, age, family size, family life cycle, income, education, occupation, religious affiliation or nationality.

4. Behaviour Segmentation - divides markets into groups based on their knowledge, attitudes, uses or responses to a product.

5. Benefits Sought - segmenting the market according to the benefits sought from products and services by certain groups of customers.

POSSIBLE CONSUMER SEGMENTS BASED ON BEHAVIOUR TOWARDS PRODUCT

SEGMENT	DESCRIPTION	DESIRED RESULTS
Current loyals	People who buy the "right" product most of all of the time	Reinforce behaviour, increase consumption, change purchase timing
Competitive loyals	People who buy a competitor's product most or all of the time	Break loyalty, persuade to switch to "right" brand
Switchers	People who buy a variety of products in the category	Persuade them to buy the "right" brand more often
Price Buyers	People who consistently buy the least expensive brand	Appeal to them with low prices or supply added value that makes price less important
Nonusers	People who don't use any product in the category	Create awareness of category and product, persuade them that product is worth buying
Usage level: heavy, medium, light *Note: these people can also be in one of the groups above.*	People who consume various levels of product in a given time period	Increase consumption or maintain high level of use.

SEGMENTATION ANALYSIS APPROACH

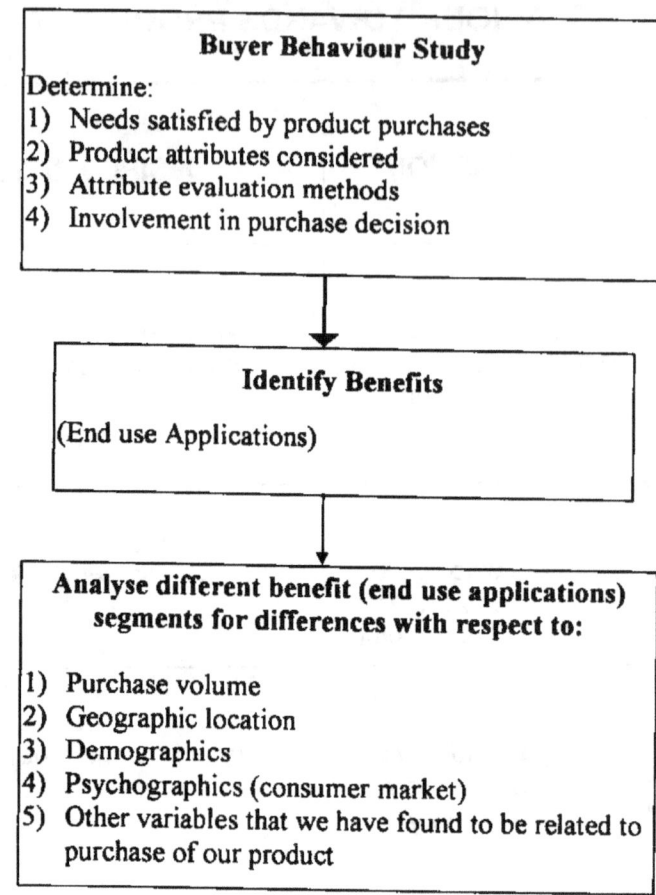

SEGMENTING BUSINESS MARKETS

1. Demographics Business markets can be segmented by industry segmentation focuses on which industries buy the product. Company size can be used. Geographic location may be used to group businesses by proximity.

2. Operating Variables Business markets can be segmented by technology (what customer technologies should we focus on?), user/nonuser status (heavy, medium, light) or customer capabilities (those needing many or few services).

3. Purchasing Approaches Five approaches are possible.
Segmentation can be by:
- Purchasing function organisation e.g. centralised or decentralised
- Power structure e.g. selecting companies controlled by a functional specialty such as technical excellence
- The nature of existing relationships e.g. current desirable customers or new desirable customers
- General purchase policies e.g. focus on companies that prefer some arrangements over others such as leasing, related support service contracts, sealed bids
- Purchasing criteria e.g. focus on criteria such as price, service or quality.

4. Situational Factors Situational segmentation may be based upon urgency (such as quick delivery needs), specific application (specific uses for the product) or size of order (few large or many small accounts).

5. Personal Characteristics Personal comparisons can lead to segmentation by buyer-seller similarity (companies with similar personnel and values), attitudes toward risk (focus on risk-taking or risk-avoiding companies) or loyalty (focus on companies that show high loyalty to their suppliers).

SEGMENTING INTERNATIONAL MARKETS
Companies typically segment international markets by geographic location, economic factors, political and legal factors or international (need similarity) factors.

REQUIREMENTS FOR EFFECTIVE SEGMENTATION
1. Measurability - refers to the degree to which the size and purchasing power of the segments can be measured.

2. Accessibility - refers to the degree to which a market segment can be reached and served.

3. Substantiality - refers to the degree to which the segments are large or profitable enough to service.

4. Actionability - is the degree to which an effective marketing program can be designed for attracting and serving segments?

SEGMENTATION STRATEGY	MARKETING MIX	TARGET MARKET
Aggregator	One Mix	All Markets
Single Segmentor	One Mix	Market A
Multiple Segmentor	Mix A Mix B Mix C	Market A Market B Market C
Combiner	Mix A	Market A & B

MARKET TARGETING

Market targeting is the process of evaluating each market segment's attractiveness and selecting one or more segments to enter.

A. EVALUATING MARKET SEGMENTS

1. **Segment Size and Growth** The company must collect and analyse data on current sales, projected sales-growth and expected profit margins for each market segment.
2. **Segment Structural Attractiveness** Long-run attractiveness includes an assessment of current and potential competitors, the threats of substitutes and the power of buyers and suppliers.
3. **Company Objectives and Resources** The company's resources and core business strengths should also fit well with the market segment opportunities.

B. SELECTING MARKET SEGMENTS

1. **Undifferentiated Marketing** This strategy uses the same marketing mix for the entire market.
2. **Differentiated Marketing** This strategy targets several market segments and designs separate marketing mixes for each of them.
3. **Concentrated Marketing** This strategy commits a company to pursue a large share of one or more submarkets.
4. **Choosing a Market-Coverage Strategy** Which strategy works best depends upon the company's resources, the degree of product variability, stage in the product life cycle, market variability and the competitors' marketing strategies.

MARKET POSITIONING

Market positioning is the process of formulating competitive positioning for a product and a detailed marketing mix. A product's position is the way the product is defined by consumers on important attributes.

Positioning Strategies

1. **Product Attributes** This positions the product on unique or distinguishing features it possesses such as a low price, unique technology, versatility or other features.
   - *Hunday: low price*
   - *Saab: performance*

2. **Benefits Offered** Positioning can be based upon the specific value provided.
   - *Crest: reduces cavities*
   - *Close-up: Confidence during close encounters*

3. **Usage Occasions** The product usage can be associated with special occasions or values e.g. *Coppertone: summer*

4. **Product Users** A product can be positioned to its most important users
   - *Everyday shampoo: for heavy users*
   - Miller Beer's heavy user positioning, "Tastes Great Less Filling"

5. **Against a Competitor** This strategy is appropriate for substitutes that cost less.

6. Away from Competitors This positions the product as unique in some respect and/or worth it e.g. *7-up the "uncola" drink*

7. Product Class The company may vary positioning as needed in relation to one or more competitors e.g. *Flora margarine vs. butter*

8. **User Class** e.g. *Baby Shampoo*

9. **Price/Quality** e.g. *Marks & Spencer (department stores)*

10. **Cultural Symbols**
    - *The Marlboro man,*
    - *Green Giant*

CHOOSING AND IMPLEMENTING A POSITIONING STRATEGY

A. IDENTIFYING POSSIBLE COMPETITIVE ADVANTAGES
1. **Product Differentiation** - can be based upon features or performance.
2. **Services Differentiation** - may come from delivery, installation, repair or training advantages.
3. **Personnel Differentiation** - is derived from a superior workforce.
4. **Image Differentiation** - can be generated from effective use of symbols in association with product consumption.

B. SELECTING THE RIGHT COMPETITIVE ADVANTAGE
1. **Unique Selling Proposition** This concept suggests that the company pick a single benefit to promote to the target market by becoming "number one" on that attribute.
2. **Underpositioning** This involves failing to ever really position the company distinctively.
3. **Overpositioning** This occurs when the company is giving the buyers too narrow a picture of the company.
4. **Confused Positioning** This occurs when the promotion messages fail to provide a clear image of the company.

C. DIFFERENCES TO PROMOTE
1. **Important** The difference must deliver a highly valued benefit to target buyers.
2. **Distinctive** Competitors do not offer the difference or the company offers the difference in a more distinctive way.
3. **Superior** The difference should be superior to other ways that customers might obtain the same benefit.
4. **Communicable** The difference is communicable and visible to buyers.
5. **Pre-emptive** Competitors cannot easily copy the difference. This may be a result of innovative technology, production economies, distribution economies and/or proprietary rights.
6. **Affordable** Buyers in the target market must be able to pay for the difference.
7. **Profitable** The difference must be profitable for the company to offer.

D. COMMUNICATING THE CHOSEN POSITION
Companies must work out the tactical details of delivering the strategy decisions to the consumer.

STEPS IN POSITIONING STRATEGY

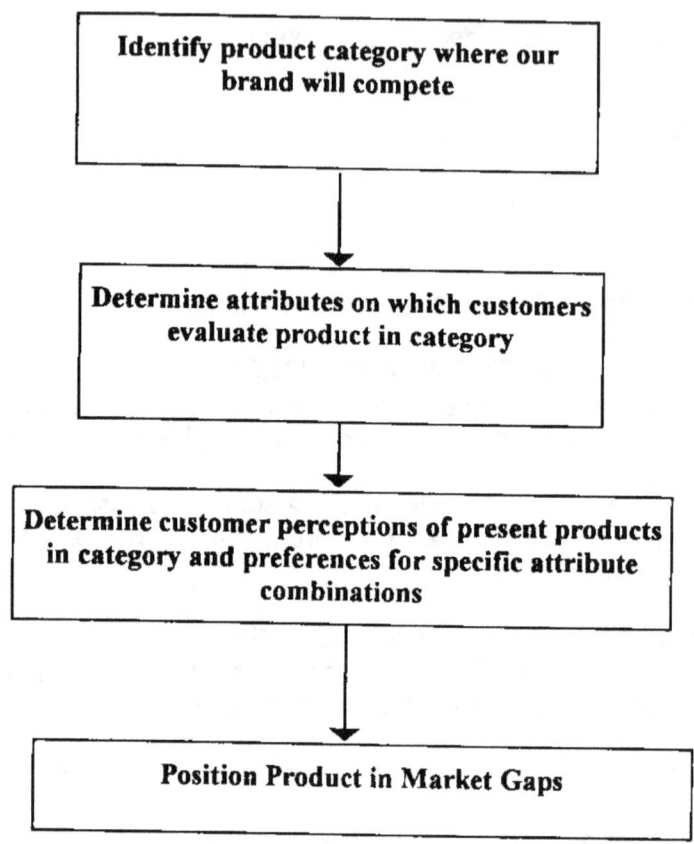

MARKETING MANAGEMENT

> TOPIC: PRODUCTS & SERVICES
> LECTURE: 9

PRODUCTS & SERVICES

WHAT IS A PRODUCT?
A product is a good, service or idea consisting of a bundle of tangible and intangible attributes that satisfies consumers and is received in exchange for money or some other unit of value.

A product is anything that can be offered to a market for attention, acquisition, use or consumption that might satisfy a need or want. Products as need satisfiers

DIFFERENCES BETWEEN GOODS AND SERVICES
Major distinguishing characteristics of a Service:
- **Intangibility** - It can not be touched, felt, smelled etc.
- **Perishability** - It cannot be stored for future sales e.g. an Airline seat, a haircut
- **Inseparability** - customer and service provider contact is often the integral part of the service e.g. Legal services/hair dresser, therefore often a direct channel of distribution.
- **Variability** in service quality lack of standardisation because services are labour intensive.

Sales of goods and services are frequently connected, i.e. a product will usually incorporate a tangible component (good) and an intangible component.

> **What are the differences between products and services?**
> We can't take inventory of services.
> - Products you have, services you perform.
> - Services are perishable.
> - Services are intangible, products are tangible.
> - It is harder to sell services than products, people negotiate.
> - New technology helps services better than its does for products.
> - Can't guarantee services.
> - Peoples' expectations of services are different.
> - Ability to charge the services according to customers' needs and capacities are greater.
> - Service quality may not be consistent.
> - You can't return services like goods.
> - Services are more specific than products.
> - Difficult to determine costs.
> - Demand fluctuates.
> - Services are inseparable - Both provider and receiver must be present.

LEVELS OF A PRODUCT

Each product item offered to customers can be viewed on three levels- the core product, the tangible or actual product and the augmented product.

1. **Core Product** - The fundamental need satisfaction that the customer is really buying

2. **Tangible or Actual Product** - the actual product is built around the core product. May have as many as five characteristics: Quality level Features Brand name Packaging all combined to carefully deliver the core benefit(s).

3. **Augmented Product** - additional consumer benefits and services e.g. Warranty, Customer training that distinguish the company's offer from competitors' offers.

4. **Potential Product** - All a product can be for a buyer through all the augmentations and transformations that the product might ultimately undergo in the future

Marketers must first identify the core consumer needs (develop core product), then design the actual product and find ways to augment it in order to create the bundle of benefits that will best satisfy the customer.

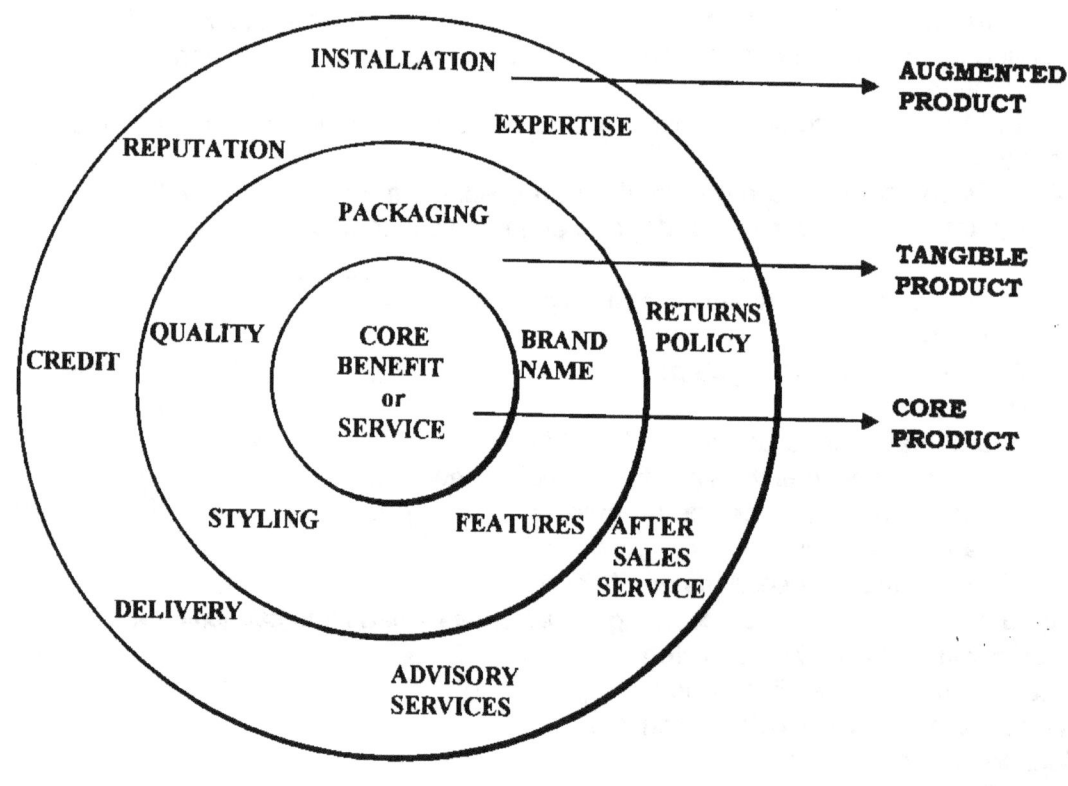

PRODUCTS CLASSIFICATIONS
Products are classified in terms of:
- the needs they satisfy
- their tangibility
- their durability
- their use

1. PRODUCT TANGIBILITY
- Tangible - **GOODS**
- Intangible - **SERVICES**

Most products have both good and service components

2. PRODUCT DURABILITY
- **Durable goods** e.g. Cars, washing machines
- **Non-durable goods** - Fast moving Consumer Goods (FMCGs) e.g. soap, beer
- **Services**

3. CONSUMER PRODUCTS AND INDUSTRIAL PRODUCTS
Products can be classified depending on who the final purchaser is.
- **Consumer products** are destined for the final consumer for personal, family and household use.
- **Industrial or Business-to-Business products**: are to satisfy the goals of the Organisation.

The same product can be purchased by both, for example a computer, for the home or the office. Components of the marketing mix will need to be changed depending on who the final purchaser is.

CONSUMER PRODUCTS
Consumer products are goods destined for use by the ultimate household consumer and in such form that they can be used without further commercial processing.
The following are classifications for consumer products:

1. CONVENIENCE GOODS: Goods that the customer usually purchases frequently, immediately and with a minimum of effort. Convenience products can be categorised into:
- Staples (e.g. bread)
- Impulse goods (not intended prior to shopping trip)
- Emergency goods (e.g. need to replace torn tights, umbrellas in the rain)

This category encompasses a wide range of household products of low unit value. Very often products in this category have low brand loyalty as the user is not prepared to go to any effort to secure supply and will accept a substitute. From this it follows that the firm must secure the widest possible availability so as to maximise sales - milk, cigarettes, chewing gum, newspapers.
Marketers need to focus on intense distribution and the time utility. Packaging is important to sell the product.

2. SHOPPING GOODS: Goods that the customer, in the process of selection and purchase, characteristically compares on such bases as suitability, quality, price and style.

Products in this group are more complex than convenience goods and exhibit a higher degree of differentiation. Usually they are purchased less frequently and are of higher unit value. Many consumer durables fall into this category.

In this category:
- Consumers expend considerable effort planning and making purchase decisions - appliances, stereos, cameras.
- Consumers are not particularly brand loyal.
- Producer/intermediary co-operation is required and as well as high margins.
- Less outlets exist than convenience goods.
- Use of sales personnel, communication of competitive advantage, branding, advertising, customer service etc.
- The product with the best set of attributes is bought (Non Price Competition).
- If product attributes are judged to be similar, then it becomes priced based.

3. SPECIALTY GOODS: Goods with unique characteristics and/or brand identification for which a significant group of buyers are habitually willing to make special purchasing efforts.
- Buyers know what they want and will usually not accept a substitute i.e. Mercedes, Nikon.
- Consumers of these products do not normally compare alternatives and are usually Brand, Store and Person loyal and will pay a premium if necessary. However they need reminder advertising.

4. UNSOUGHT GOODS: Goods that consumers are unaware of or know about but do not normally think of buying e.g. life insurance, funeral plots, encyclopaedias, kitchen utensil sets, dental work. The need arises when there are sudden problems to resolve.

BUSINESS-TO-BUSINESS OR INDUSTRIAL GOODS

A **Business Market** is a market consisting of businesses, individuals or organizations that purchase products or services to use in the production of other products and services, in their day-to-day operations or for resale.

Business Marketing The marketing efforts directed at any consuming group other than ultimate consumers.

TYPES OF BUSINESS MARKETS
1. **Vendor** - marketer who sells to a business customer.
2. **Manufacturers** produce goods that are then sold to wholesalers, retailers, governments, institutions and to ultimate consumers. May purchase every type of business-to-business product except goods for resale.
3. **Wholesalers** - buy goods and services from manufacturers and other wholesalers and resell to other wholesalers and retailers. Provide transportation and storage of goods.
4. **Retailers** sell goods and services to ultimate consumers.
5. **Government Markets** include local, regional and national governments. Typically engage in formal buying process and typically award contracts to lowest bidder.
6. **Institutional Markets** are customers who serve the needs of large groups of people in institutional settings i.e. they have people under their care such as schools, hospitals and prisons. May be government owned, not-for-profit or for-profit organizations.
7. **Small Businesses** More likely to be retailers and the purchasing process is typically less formalized

DIFFERENCES BETWEEN THE BUSINESS AND THE CONSUMER MARKET

1. **DEMAND**
   - **Derived demand** - demand for one product that arises from the demand for another product. The demand for many business products is derived from the demand for consumer goods e.g. the auto industry's demand for tires is a function of the consumer's demand for cars. Marketers must consider derived demand when planning their marketing strategies.
   - **Inelastic demand** an increase or decrease in the price of an item will not have much impact on business's demand for it. Inelasticity occurs at the industry-wide level. Individual marketers must be price competitive.

2. **MARKET SIZE** The business market typically has fewer, larger customers who are sometimes geographically concentrated.

3. **PROMOTIONAL TECHNIQUES** Personal selling tends to dominate promotion. Advertising tends to be through magazines and trade journals.

4. **NUMBER OF INDIVIDUALS INVOLVED** Many individuals are usually involved in the purchase decision and exert influence in business purchases - Decision Making Unit (DMU)

5. **BUYER EXPERTISE AND RATIONALITY** As professional buyers, business buyers are more knowledgeable and rational, use detailed specifications, are concerned about quality and rarely engage in impulse buying. However, they are influenced by both rational considerations and emotional needs.

6. **SERVICE IS IMPORTANT** A product marketed to organizational buyers is generally less standardized and level of service that accompanies it is important - usually more important than price.

7. **DISTRIBUTION CHANNELS ARE SHORTER** In business marketing, distribution channels are shorter

8. **CUSTOMER RELATIONSHIPS TEND TO BE LONG-TERM.**
   - **Relationship Marketing** - developing a relationship between a marketer and his or her customers so that marketing activity becomes part of a continuing interaction between the two.
   - **Strategic Alliance** - an enduring relationship between a business marketer and a customer that represents a planned, mutual effort to solve problems and meet the needs of the customer.

CLASSIFICATIONS FOR INDUSTRIAL PRODUCTS

Industrial Products are goods which are destined for use in producing other goods or rendering services, as contrasted with goods destined to be sold to ultimate consumers.

Certain goods which fall into this category may also be classified as consumer goods, e.g. sugar, computers, chairs, diesel fuel, etc. Where such an overlap exists, the purpose for which the product is bought determines its classification.

Industrial products fall into 5 major categories:

1. MATERIALS AND PARTS

Those industrial materials which in part or in whole become a part of the final product but which have undergone no more processing than is required for convenience, protection, economy in storage, transportation or handling. These are typically purchased by OEMs (Original Equipment Manufacturers) and other manufacturers.

a. Raw Materials
- **Farm products** - food crops, milk, natural rubber
- **Natural products** - products mined or produced by extractive industries for use, with little or no alteration, in the production of other goods e.g. coal, crude oil, timber, natural rubber and crushed ore.

b. Manufactured materials and parts
- **Processed materials** - These are industrial goods which become a part of the finished product and which have undergone processing beyond that required for raw materials but not so much as finished parts. Steel, plastic moulding powders, cement, flour, chemicals, sheet metal, plastics and specialty steel fit this description. They are typically produced to the specifications of the customer.
- **Component parts** - goods that are incorporated into other manufactured products with little or no change. e.g. transistors, small electric motors, switches. These are usually sold to OEMs and repair facilities

2. CAPITAL ITEMS

Long-lasting goods that facilitate developing and/or managing the finished product. They do not become part of the physical product and are exhausted only after repeated use.

a. Installations
- **Buildings** - Factories, Offices, Warehouses
- **Heavy Equipment** - products that are used directly in the production of other goods and are often attached to the physical plant of the businesses using them e.g. bottling equipment, printing presses, blast furnaces, boilers, presses, power lathes, bank vaults. This equipment may be purchased or leased.

b. Light or Accessory Equipment
- goods that are required in order for individuals in the firm to "get the job done" but are not permanently affixed to the physical plant. This equipment may be purchased or leased.
- **Portable factory equipment** - power tools, cars
- **Office / Accessory Equipment** - Typewriters, personal computers, fax machines

3. SUPPLIES - goods that are consumed by a business in its day-to-day operations. They do not become a part of the physical product or are continually exhausted in facilitating the operation of an enterprise. They may be referred to as MRO products (Maintenance, Repair and Operating products).
    a. Operating supplies - Consumable Supplies: business stationery, forms, pencils, computer disks.
    b. Maintenance and repair items - cleaning compounds, drill bits, oils.

4. BUSINESS SERVICES - all services purchased by businesses.
    a. Maintenance and repair services e.g. machinery, computers
    b. Business advisory services e.g. Financial, legal, marketing research etc.

5. GOODS FOR RESALE - products purchased by wholesalers and retailers for resale to other wholesalers, retailers and ultimate consumers with no alteration to the product e.g. clothing, frozen foods, toys.

Although few producers give much thought to actually classifying their output along the above lines, this is probably due to the fact that their product line falls within a single category and not because there is no value in developing such a classification. In fact the product category has a fundamental effect on the firm's marketing strategy as a whole, as well as having far-reaching implications for its internal organisation and operation.

MARKETING MANAGEMENT

TOPIC: PRODUCT STRATEGIES
LECTURE: 10

PRODUCT STRATEGIES

A firm's product policy is fundamental to the whole operation of the business. Most new companies are conceived to produce a specific product or group of products and it is this decision which dictates the industry to which they will belong, the markets they will serve and the nature and extend of the resources, methods and techniques they will employ.

Product Planning is the systematic decision making related to all aspects of the development and management of a firms products including branding and packaging.
Product strategy calls for making co-ordinated decisions on product items, product lines and the product mix.

ELEMENTS OF A PRODUCT MIX

If an Organisation is marketing more than one product it has a product mix.
- **Product item** - a single product
- **Product line** - all items of the same type
- **Product mix** - total group of products that an Organisation markets

Product Depth measures the number of products that are offered within each product line. It satisfies several consumer segments for the same product, maximises shelf space, discourages competitors, covers a range of prices and sustains dealer support. However there is a high cost in inventory etc.
Product Width measures the number of product lines a company offers. It enables a firm to diversify products and appeal to different consumer needs and encourages one stop shopping.

PRODUCT POSITIONING AND PRODUCT REPOSITIONING

Positioning refers to the place a product offering occupies in consumers' minds on important attributes, relative to competing offerings. It is how new and current items in the product mix are perceived, in the minds of the consumer.
- New Product - need to communicate benefits
- Established Products - need to reinforce benefits

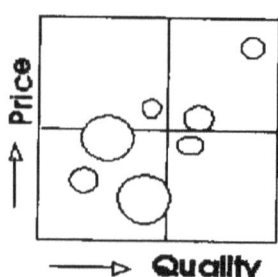

One way of examining position is to compare quality to price. Other variables can be used in the analysis, such as warranty, life expectancy and service.

There is no universal best position to occupy.

Positioning is based on the organization's capability, the market need and differentiation from the competitive offerings.

Repositioning - Existing products that are targeted to new markets or market segments

Ideal Characteristics
Marketers need to introduce products that possess characteristics that the target market desires most and considers ideal. Product positioning is crucial here.
- **Consumers desires** refer to the attributes consumers would like the products to possess
- **Ideal points**. Whenever a group of consumers has a distinctive "ideal" for a product category they represent a potential target market segment.

A firm does well if the attributes of the product are perceived by consumers as being close to their ideal. The objective is to be "more ideal" than the competitors. Each product must provide some unique combination of new features desired by the target market. Instead of allowing the customer to position products independently, marketers try to influence and shape consumers' concepts and perceptions.

New Product Positioning
When developing a new product, a company should:
1. Identify all the features that are offered by all its major competitors.
2. Identify important features/benefits used in making purchase decisions.
3. Determine the overall ranking of features by importance and relate the importance of each feature to its "uniqueness".

WHAT ARE NEW PRODUCTS?
- Original products: New-to-the-World Products that create and entirely new market
- Additional SKUs (Stock Keeping Unit)
- Improved products
- Modified products
- New brands

Developing new products is expensive and risky.
Failure to introduce new products is also risky.

NEED TO DEVELOP NEW PRODUCTS
Failure to develop new products exposes company to risk. Existing products are vulnerable to:
- changing consumer needs and tastes
- new technologies
- shortened product life cycles
- increased domestic and foreign competition

Why are new products successful?
- Provide greater value than competitive products
- Buyers perceive that their needs will be met better than with the purchase of competitive products

Why do new products fail?
- Managerial intransigence
- Market size is overestimated
- Product is not well designed
- Incorrectly positioned
- Not advertised effectively
- Overpriced

- New product development costs higher than expected
- Competitors fight back harder than expected

THE CONCEPT OF THE PRODUCT LIFE CYCLE

- The PRODUCT LIFE CYCLE (PLC) is graphical portrayal of customer acceptance of a product, industry, product model, brand etc. In many ways the life of a product resembles the human life cycle with its phases of birth, growth, maturity, senility and death and has given rise to the concept of the product life cycle

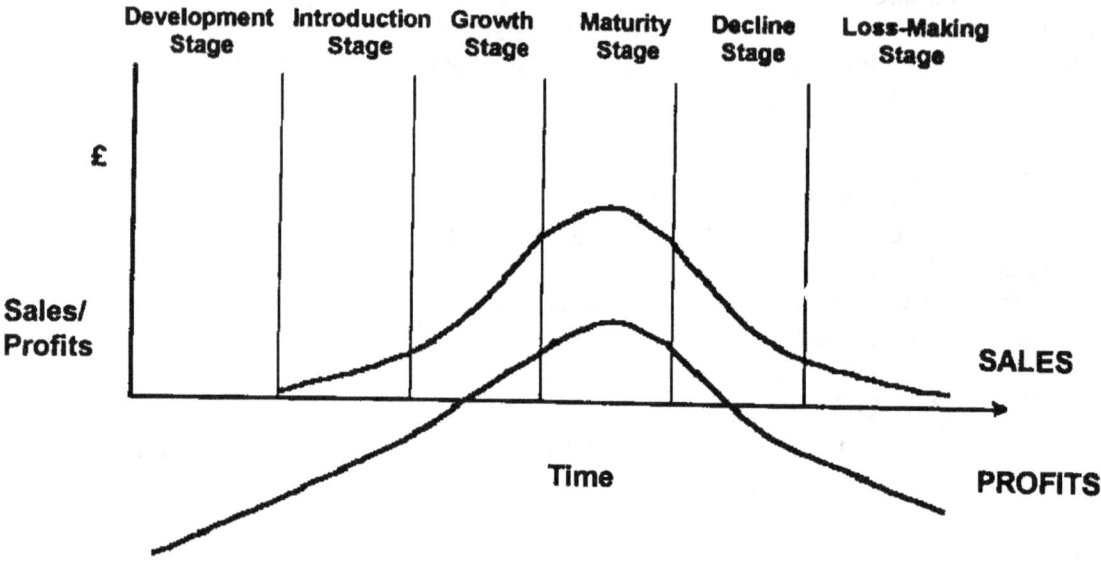

The first stage in the PLC is the development stage followed by the product introduction into the market. Assuming survival, new products enjoy a period of increasing demand and growth. In time, other new products will enter the market offering advantages over the now mature product, which will experience a decline in demand as consumers switch their allegiance. The length of any of the phases of the product life cycle can not be predicted.

NEW DEVELOPMENTS

Following years of research and observation Theo Hadjiyannis Director General of The Cyprus Institute of Marketing has found out that two new stages on the PLC can be deduced. These are the:

- **Development stage** i.e. before even the product is dynamically introduced into the market and considered a commercial entity and the
- **Loss-Making Stage** which is the stage where the product remains in the market place but at an inactive state and the company makes losses. The reasons why the company maintains the product in the market despite its profit losses might be several:
    1. **Ignorance or inaccurate data**
    2. **Sentimental reasons.**
    3. **Belief that the situation may be reversed.**
    4. **Customer Loyalty.**

Examples of such products might be exclusive products appealing to a small segment of the population such as very special types of drugs, cosmetics, tobacco, special blend of alcoholic beverages, etc.

From the observations of Theo Hadjiyannis in the last 15 years of Cypriot companies only 5% - 10% of the products of a company are profit makers.

MARKETING STRATEGY THROUGHOUT THE PLC

By monitoring changes in demand marketers can predict the onset of growth, maturity and decline and vary their marketing inputs accordingly. For example, reduce the level of advertising expenditures during growth and emphasise production and physical distribution, step up the amount of sales promotion at the onset of maturity, retire the product when decline sets in etc.

1. **INTRODUCTORY STAGE**
   - Marketing objectives: create product awareness and trial
   - Product strategy: offer a basic model product, tight quality control
   - Pricing strategy: depends upon objectives:
     - use penetration-pricing policy if market share is the objective
     - use skimming policy if high revenue is the objective
   - Distribution: build selective distribution
   - Advertising: build product awareness among early adopters and dealers; stimulate primary demand
   - Sales promotion: use heavy sales promotion to stimulate product trial

2. **GROWTH STAGE**
   - Marketing objectives: maximise market share
   - Product strategy: offer product extensions, additional models to reach other market segments and to counteract competitive entries
   - Pricing strategy: often a penetrating strategy
   - Distribution: build as intensive distribution as possible for product category
   - Advertising: build awareness and interest; stimulate selective demand
   - Sales promotion: reduce since consumer demand should be building

3. **MATURITY STAGE**
   - Marketing objectives: defend market share, maximise profits
   - Product strategy: diversify brand and models
   - Pricing strategy: match or beat competitors
   - Distribution: build strong relationships with dealers, keep intensive distribution
   - Advertising: stress brand differences and benefits
   - Sales promotion: increase to encourage brand switching

4. **DECLINE STAGE**
   - Marketing objectives: reduce expenditures and "milk" the brand for maximum financial gain
   - Product strategy: phase out weak models
   - Pricing strategy: match or beat competition
   - Distribution: phase out unprofitable dealers
   - Advertising: reduce to level necessary to maintain profitable sales
   - Sales promotion: reduce to minimal level

PROACTIVE MARKETING STRATEGY is utilised during the introductory and sales growth stages. The emphasis is on communication, attempting to stimulate both primary and selective demand.

REACTIVE MARKETING STRATEGY often occurs in the maturity stage when market share stabilises, private brands appear, profits begin to drop and emphasis often shifts to sales promotions. Marketing strategy during the maturity stage should remain proactive;

however, the emphasis often turns to product improvements, new product development, etc. in an effort to prolong the product life cycle. The result is that major competitors tend to react to the industry leader's marketing initiatives.

THE ROLE OF NEW PRODUCT DEVELOPMENT

Although it is impossible to predict the life span of a given product there is an inevitable certainty that it will eventually be replaced by the introduction of a new substitute or even made totally obsolete as the result of technological innovations

Thus a relatively minor change in a product's composition or marketing may assume major significance in the user's eyes and result in a marked shift in demand for that product. It is argued, therefore, that branding can only succeed as a competitive strategy given the existence of perceived differences. If this is so it follows that a competitive market will be characterised by a continual effort to develop such differences.

Marketers who succeed in distinguishing their products from that of their competitors through the creation of a new and desirable attribute will enjoy an advantage which will enable them to expand their sales and share of market. Such an advantage is in the nature of a monopoly, which may last for years if protected by a patent, e.g. the Polaroid camera and film or be eroded overnight by imitative innovation, e.g. enzyme active detergents. The role of new product development is the creation of such competitive advantages.

THE IMPORTANCE OF NEW PRODUCTS

Any attempt to measure the contribution of new products to a firm's or industry's growth and profitability is bedevilled by the lack of consensus as to what constitutes a new product. Similar difficulties also exist when one seeks to measure the failure rate of new product introductions.

Two valid generalisations may be advanced:
1. Firms are increasingly dependent upon new products for the maintenance and expansion of sales.
2. Many new product introductions are failures in the sense that they do not achieve the expected sales level and are withdrawn from the market.

ALTERNATIVE NEW PRODUCT STRATEGIES

Relatively few new products emanate from totally new companies and attention here will be focused on the established firm with an existing product line. Such firms vary in their willingness to innovate and develop new products and are usually categorised as leaders and followers. Whether a firm is a leader or a follower, there are several distinct ways in which it can add to its product line which may be summarised as:

1. **Modification of an existing product**, e.g. addition of a new ingredient in a detergent, toothpaste or cake mix, increase in the cubic capacity of a car engine or offer a saloon-based van etc.

2. **Addition of a complementary product**, e.g. a new brand of light cigarettes, a new flavour in food or beverage e.g. caffeine-free Coke, the development of a new 4x4 car model.

3. **Entry into an existing market which is new to the firm**, e.g. Cadbury's entry into the cake market, the Parker Pen Company entry to the financial services market.

4. **Development of a new market through the introduction of a totally new product**, e.g. mobile telephones, CD players, notebook computers, video cameras.

These alternatives are listed in ascending order of risk.
- The first strategy usually entails a low level of risk and is frequently in response to overt public demand. Thus, offering a van-version of a saloon car model or offering a fuel injection system can extend the competitive positioning of a car and requires little additional investment.
- The second strategy involves a greater degree of risk, as the firm has no previous direct experience of the production and marketing of the new item.
- The third strategy involves entering a new market with all the dangers inherent to an unknown territory.
- The fourth alternative exposes the firm to a completely unknown situation, added to which the value of fundamentally new products may take years to establish owing to the innate conservatism of the potential user.

NEW PRODUCT DEVELOPMENT

Despite the risks involved, new product development is a competitive necessity and has prompted many companies to evolve formalised procedures for dealing with the complexities and uncertainties inherent in the process. Such procedures will normally include:
1. Location and screening of new product ideas.
2. Evaluation of market potential and possible contribution to the firm's overall objectives.
3. Prototype development and product testing.
4. Test marketing.

Many new product development procedures distinguish additional stages, but these tend to be a more detailed statement of the basic steps outlined above.

1. THE LOCATION AND SCREENING OF NEW PRODUCT IDEAS

To be effective, any search for new product ideas should be structured in the sense that efforts should be directed towards a specific area and pursued systematically. Most firms possess some special skill or distinctive competence and it is this that they should seek to exploit in developing new products.

The adoption of search criteria is essential if the firm is to avoid wasteful exploration of the multiplicity of sources open to it. Such sources may be internal or external to the firm.

- **Internally**, every member of the company is a potential source of new product ideas and company suggestion schemes have thrown up many more valuable suggestions than they are generally credited with. Many companies now have their own Research and Development Department, specifically charged with developing in-house projects, in addition to which Sales, Marketing and Production usually have distinct ideas of how the current product line could be improved or extended.

- **Externally**, the firm's distributors and customers are frequently a fruitful source of ideas, as are the product offerings of one's competitors.

Such criteria usually require that
- The product will meet a clearly defined consumer need.
- The product is consistent with the firm's production and marketing policies.
- The product will utilise the firm's existing skills and resources.
- The product will contribute to the firm's long-run profitability.

Utilising this data, the marketing department can then develop its own estimate of the costs associated with varying levels of market penetration.

2. FINANCIAL CONSIDERATIONS

New product introductions represent an investment opportunity for the firm and it is essential that such opportunities be evaluated in the light of all other possible uses of the firm's resources. In the normal course of events a company is faced with a disparate collection of investment opportunities and so must develop a common denominator with which it may rank dissimilar projects in order of preference. The discounted cash flow (D.C.F.) technique has been widely adopted for this purpose.

The basic principle upon which the D.C.F. technique is based in recognition of the fact that a currently available sum of money can be invested to generate a stream of future earnings. This £1.00 invested today will be worth £1.10 a year hence if the return on investment is 10 per cent per annum. Conversely, £1 received a year hence is only worth £0.909 today if it could be invested at 10 per cent. By applying the D.C.F. technique one can make direct comparisons of investment opportunities with very dissimilar future cash flows and select the one with the highest net present value.

3. TESTING THE PRODUCT CONCEPT

a. Prototype Development

Given the revised short-list the next step is a detailed feasibility study based on tests of the product concept. Such tests may have been made already, but if not, it is essential that they be undertaken prior to detailed market studies and the finalisation of prototypes.
In some instances the product concept is too complex to be tested verbally and some form of mock-up or prototype must be used to.

Once the product concept has been validated, a detailed market study should be undertaken. If it is subsequently decided to market the product, this study will form the basis of the marketing plan.

Concurrently the engineering and production departments will develop final prototypes and decide on the production techniques to be used if the project is adopted.

b. Product Testing

In view of the high risks associated with new product introductions, field-testing should logically precede firm commitment to large-scale production and marketing. Product testing consists of an objective appraisal of the product's performance, free of subjective associations created by other elements of the marketing mix e.g. price, packaging, brand image etc. It should not be confused with test marketing, which includes consideration of these factors.

Certain product attributes are capable of precise measurement, e.g. the efficiency of an engine, the life of an electric light bulb, whereas other depend upon consumer preference and defy exact quantification, e.g. the taste of food or beverage.

4. TEST MARKETING

Basically, test marketing consists of launching the product on a limited scale in a representative market, thus avoiding the costs of a full-scale launch while permitting the collection of market data, which may subsequently be used for predictive purposes.

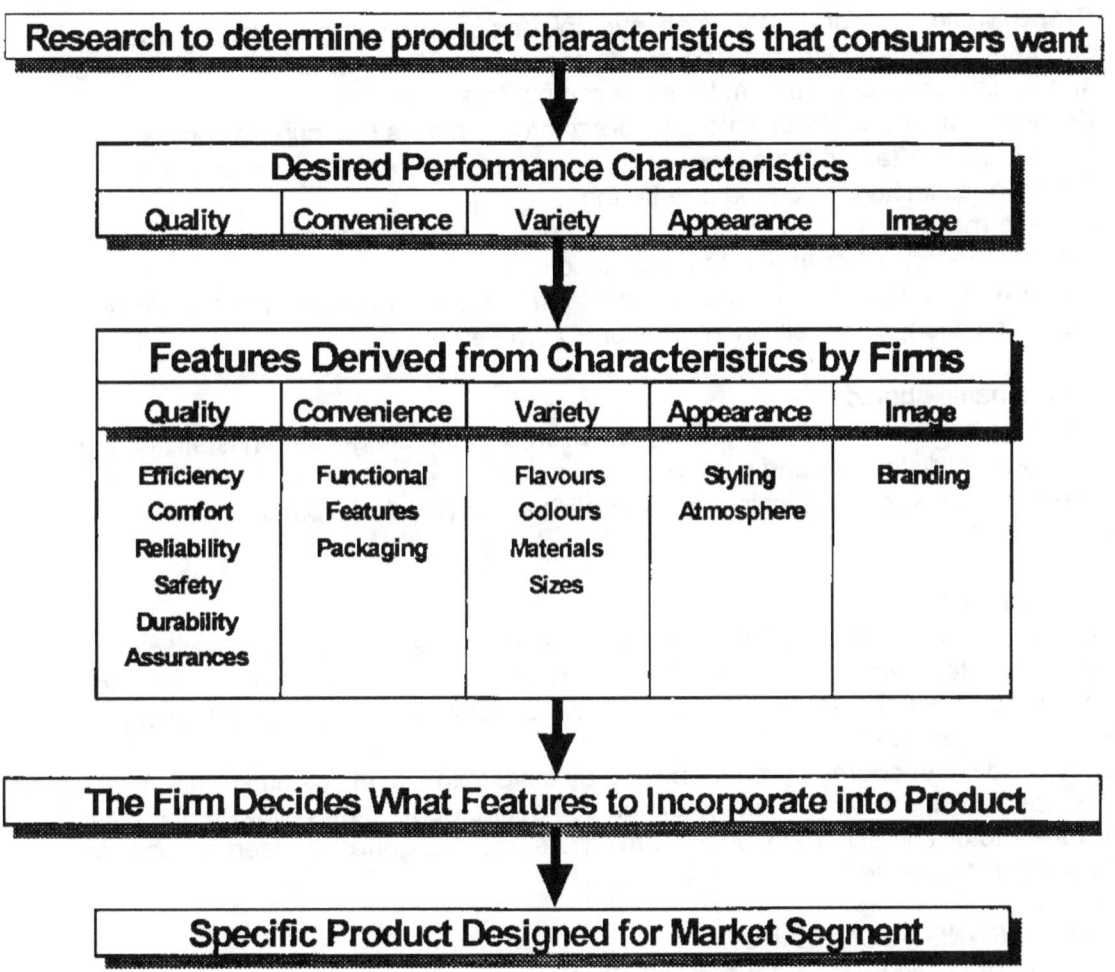

MARKETING MANAGEMENT

TOPIC: BRANDING & PACKAGING
LECTURE: 11

BRANDING

Branding is the use of a name, term, symbol or design or a combination of these to identify a product. Branding can be characterised by a brand name or a trademark. Branding is useful to the customer as well as to the firm. Since brands have different level of acceptance, brand selection is a key issue handled with the help of specific branding strategies.

- **Brand** Name, term or phrase, sign, symbol, design or a combination of these denoters, intended to identify the goods or services of one seller or group of sellers and to differentiate them from those of competitors
- **Brand name** - consists of words, letters and/or numbers that can be vocalised
- **Brand mark** (often called a logo) - that part that appears in the form of a symbol, design or distinctive colouring or lettering
- **Service mark** - a symbol, design or a group of distinctive letters that designate a service offering rather than a tangible good.
- **Trademark** - a registered brand, a legal term indicating exclusive right. It offers legal protection, especially in international commerce.

A good brand name should:
- Describe the product benefits e.g. Easy Off-oven cleaner; cling-free (antistatic drying)
- Be memorable, distinctive and positive
- Fit with competition or product image (Sharp for audio/visual equipment).
- Have no legal restrictions.

BRANDING FUNCTIONS

Branding is important because it helps customers to identify a product with specific attributes associated with it such as need suitability, quality, standards, social acceptance etc. It constitutes a benchmark that assures regular satisfaction and makes shopping feasible and more efficient.

On the firm's side, it encourages repeat buying by developing loyal customers and thus brings the cost down, resulting in an increased competing edge. It has allowed particular manufacturers to distinguish themselves from others and has generally been a significant factor in building corporate image.

LEVELS OF BRAND ACCEPTANCE

Five levels of brand acceptance are currently identified
1. **Non-recognition** of brand denotes unfamiliarity with a given brand
2. **Brand recognition** denotes a certain familiarity with a given brand by a set of customers.
3. **Brand preference** implies that the customer prefers a particular brand over others because of perceived reasons.
4. **Brand insistence** connotes a willingness on the part of the consumer to make an effort to get the chosen brand.
5. **Rejection** can be the result of a negative image or inappropriate market target.

BRANDING STRATEGY

Since branding decision has implications in terms of customers' perception, brand selection should not be a random exercise. Brand names and trademarks ought to be devoted particular attention in order to capture as large a portion of the market as possible. Brand strategy is an intimate aspect of product strategy. A marketer has to decide:

1. Which products to brand (brand-sponsor decisions)
2. How to brand them (brand-quality decisions, multibrand decisions and brand-family decisions)
3. How to manage the brands (brand-extension strategy and brand-repositioning decisions).

ADVANTAGES AND DISADVANTAGES OF DIFFERENT BRAND STRATEGIES

	Individual Brand Names for all Product Items.	One Brand Name for All Product Items
PROS	1. Success/Failure of one product does not affect success of other product items. 2. Easier to create unique identities for product items. 3. At retail level, may help the marketer capture more shelf space.	1. Development cost is less 2. Customer goodwill toward established brands transfers to new brands making new product development easier.
CONS	1. Development cost higher 2. No goodwill for new product introductions.	1. Success/failure of one product item may affect other product items. 2. Harder to create unique identities for product items. 3. May be harder to gain shelf space at retail level.

The first of several decisions in brand strategy is whether the company should even put a brand name on one or more of its products. The alternative to branding is simply to sell the product in bulk to middlemen or the final customer. Until recently, most staple products like sugar, salt, bacon, cloth went unbranded. Producers shipped their goods to middlemen who would sell them out of barrels, bins or cases without any identification of the supplier. Only finer goods were branded in some cases. Reasons for Not Branding may be:

- Unable or unwilling to promote and maintain consistent quality
- Cannot be physically differentiated from other firms' products

THE BRAND DECISION

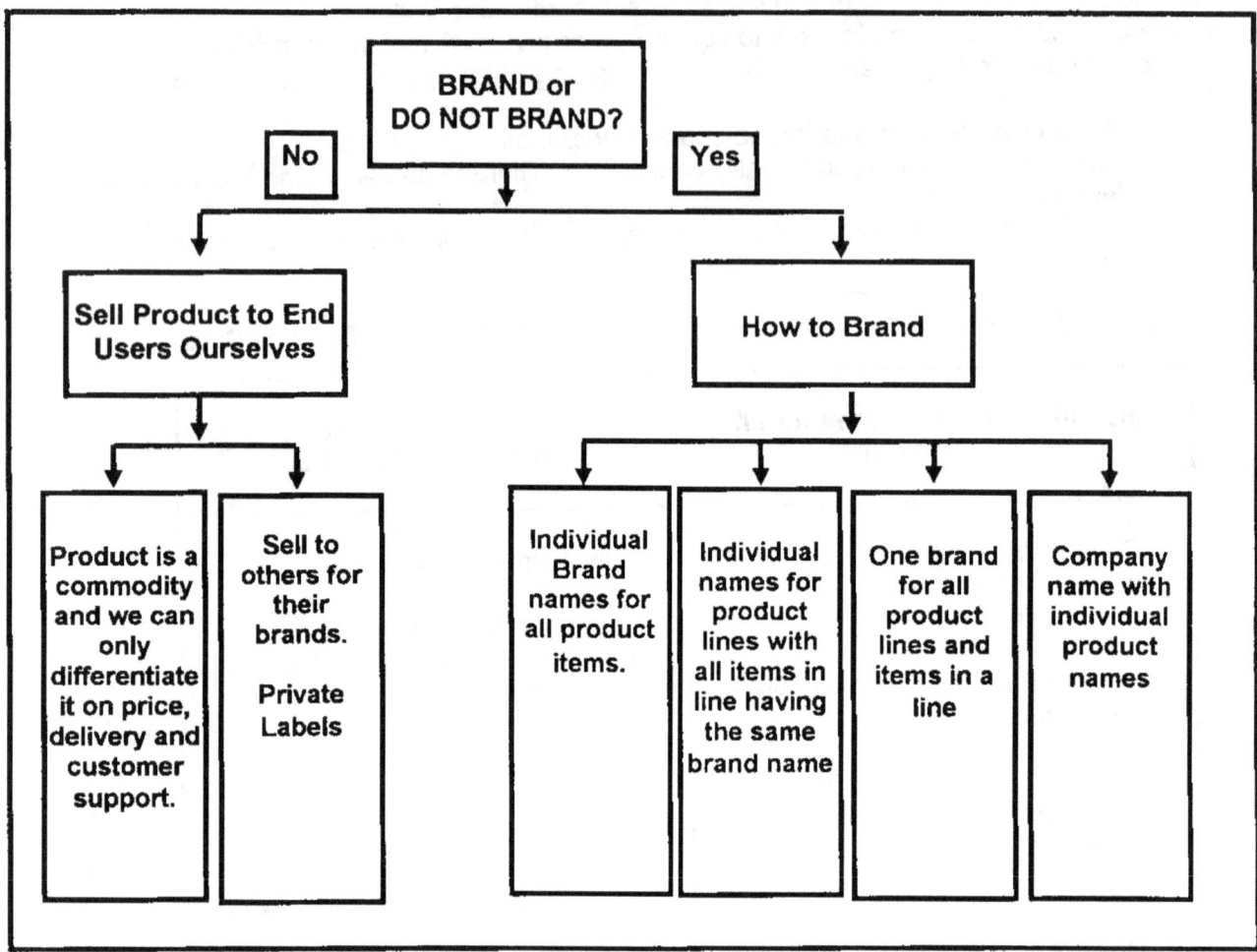

1. BRAND-SPONSOR DECISION

In branding, producers may use their own name (manufacturer brand), middlemen's names or follow a mixed-brand policy, producing some output under their own name and some output under middlemen's names.

Types of Brand
- **Manufacturer's (national) brand**
- **Private brand** (middleman, distributor or store brand).
- **Generic products** (no brand) -those product sold with no identification other than the contents of the package. Generally of lower and/or inconsistent quality

Although manufacturer brands tend to dominate in the market, middlemen are often able to make a profit because they do not bear the manufacturers' heavy promotional expenses.

On the other hand, when middlemen introduce their own brands, it gives them more control over pricing and some measure of control over suppliers. Thus, middlemen's brands have become an important factor in brand competition.

Furthermore, retail shelf space is scarce and many manufacturers, especially newer and smaller ones, cannot introduce products into distribution under their own name. Middlemen take special care to maintain the quality of their brands, building consumers' confidence. Many buyers know the private label brand is often manufactured by one of the larger manufacturers anyway.

Middlemen's brands are often price lower than comparable manufacturers' brands, thus appealing to budget-conscious shoppers, especially in times of recession. Middlemen give more prominent display to their own brands and make sure they are better stocked. For these and other reasons, the former dominance of the manufacturers' brands is weakening. Indeed, some marketing commentators predict that the middlemen's brands will eventually knock out all but the strongest manufacturer brands.

Factors that encourage manufacturers to produce distributor brands
 a. Product class is beyond mid-point of PLC.
 b. Product is approaching commodity status.
 c. Reseller is more important than manufacturer in assuring quality and/or style or has more economic power i.e. Increasing power of resellers
 d. Competitors offer distributor' brands.
 e. Economic downturns cause consumers to become more price conscious.
 f. Distributor's volume is sufficient to permit customisation.

2. BRAND-QUALITY DECISION
In developing a brand, the manufacturer has to establish the brand's quality level and other attributes that will support the brand's targeted position in the marketplace. Quality is one of the major positioning tools of the marketer. Manufacturers do not all attempt to build the highest-quality products. Higher-quality products will cost consumers more. There will be markets for each quality level.

Each manufacturer faces two decisions:
- Where to locate the brand's initial quality and
- How to manage the brand's quality level through time.

Most brands can be established initially at one of four quality levels: low, average, above average and superior. Since it has been shown that although profitability tends to increase as quality improves from low to average and above average quality, it levels off as quality reaches its peak. This suggests that companies should aim to deliver above-average quality. Superior quality increases profitability only slightly, while inferior quality hurts profitability substantially. Furthermore, high marketing expenditures tend not to compensate for inferior product quality. It doesn't pay to promote a poor product.

3. FAMILY-BRAND DECISIONS
Manufacturers who choose to produce most of their output under their own name still face several choices.
At least four brand-name strategies can be distinguished:
 a. **Individual brand names.**
 b. **A blanket family name for all products.**
 c. **Separate family names for all products.**
 d. **A company trade name combined with individual product names.**

a. Individual Brand-Names Decision Competitors within the same industry may adopt quite different brand name strategies. The advantage of individual brand-name strategy is that the company does not tie its reputation to the product's acceptance. If the product fails, it is not a bad mark for the manufacturer. Or if the new product is of lower quality, the company does not dilute its reputation. The manufacturer of a line of expensive watches or high-quality food products can introduce lower-quality lines without using its own name. On the positive side the individual-brand-names strategy permits the firm to search for the best name for each new product. Another advantage is that a new name permits the building of new excitement and conviction. e.g. P&G - Pampers, Crest

b. Blanket Family Decision The opposite policy, that of using a blanket family name for all products, also has some advantages if the manufacturer is willing to maintain quality for all items in the line. The cost of introducing the product will be less because there is no need for "name" research or for expensive advertising to create brand-name recognition and preference. Furthermore, sales will be strong if the manufacturer's name is good. e.g. HEINZ -Spaghetti, Baked Beans etc.

c. Separate Family Names Decision Where a company produces or sells quite different types of products, it may not be appropriate to use one blanket family name. Different family brand names may be attributed to different quality lines within the same product class.

d. Company Trade name Decision Some manufacturers want to associate their company name along with an individual brand for each product. In these cases, the company name legitimises and the individual name individualises the new product. e.g. Honda - Prelude, Civic

4. BRAND EXTENSION STRATEGY
A brand-extension strategy is any effort to use a successful brand name to launch product modifications or additional products. Another kind of brand extension occurs when durable-goods manufacturers add stripped-down models to the lower end of their line in order to advertise their brand as starting at a low price.

5. MULTIBRAND DECISION
A multibrand strategy is the development by a particular seller of two or more brands that compete with each other. There are several reasons why manufacturers turn to multibrand strategy.
a. First, there is the severe battle for shelf space in supermarkets. Each brand that the distributors accept gets some allocation of shelf space. By introducing several brands a manufacturer ties up more of the available shelf space, leaving less for competitors.
b. Second, few consumers are so loyal to a brand that they won't occasionally try another. They respond to cents-off deals, gifts and new-product entries that claim superior performance. The manufacturer who never introduces another brand entry will almost inevitably face a declining market share. The only way to capture the "brand switchers" is to be on the offering end of a new brand.
c. Finally, creating new brands develops excitement and encourages efficiency within the manufacturer's organisation.

Multibrand Disadvantage - A major pitfall in introducing a number of multibrand entries, is that each obtains only a small share of the market and is not particularly profitable. In this case, the company has spread its resources over several partially successful brands instead of concentrating on a few brands and building each one up to highly profitable levels. Such companies should weed out the weaker brands and establish tighter screening procedures for choosing new brands to introduce. Ideally, a company's brands should cannibalise the competitors' brands and not each other.

6. BRAND-REPOSITIONING DECISION

However well a brand is initially positioned in a market, a number of circumstances may call for repositioning thinking:

a. A competitor may have placed its brand next to the company's brand, thus cutting into its market share in that segment.
b. Customer preferences may have shifted, leaving the company's brand less in the centre of a preference cluster.
c. New customer preference clusters may have formed that represent attractive opportunities.

THE IMPORTANCE OF BRANDS

- in 1990, 62% of all consumers said they buy only "well known" brand names
- in 1990, 61% of all consumers said that they regard brands as an "assurance of quality"

Brand image - the way the product/company is defined by the consumer. It is based upon consumer experience with the product/company, both actual and perceived.

Brand equity Refers to the added value that a certain brand name gives to a product. It is based upon:
- the degree of brand loyalty
- brand awareness
- quality perceptions
- patents and trademarks
- extent of distribution

BUILDING BRAND EQUITY
- Differentiation - ability to stand apart
- Relevance - the real and perceived importance to a large consumer segment
- Esteem - perceived quality and popularity of the brand
- Knowledge - awareness and understanding

Brand preferences have declined in the last year for: groceries, sporting goods, consumer electronics, hardware, housewares and computer hardware.

Consumers seek national brands when shopping for cosmetics, cameras, soft drinks, toys and film.

PACKAGING

The basic function of any pack is to protect its contents in transit, in storage and in use. This criterion will play a major role in determining the shape, size and materials used, but in recent years there has been a tendency to subordinate such practical aspects to design and promotional considerations.

In most cases there will be little or no conflict between the physical characteristics considered desirable by manufacturers and distributors and the promotional and design elements demanded by consumers. However it will be useful to consider the requirements of these two groups separately to emphasise the varying nature of their needs.

Packaging is the general group of activities in product planning that involves designing and producing the container or wrapper for a product. Packaging is obviously closely related to labelling and branding because the label appears on the package and the brand is typically on the label.

The 3 main reasons for Packaging are:

1. To protect the product on its route from the manufacturer to the final consumer.

2. To implement a firm's marketing program.
   - It helps to identify a product and thus prevent substitution of competitive goods. It promotes and sells the product.
   - It is the most significant way in which a firm can differentiate its products from competitive offerings.
   - By changing the package a change in the product is implied.

3. Packaging may be used to increase profit possibilities:
   - Customers may pay more just to get the special package even though the rise in price exceeds the cost of the package.

DISTRIBUTOR REQUIREMENTS
Pack design will depend very largely on the:
1. Nature of the contents in terms of their value, physical composition and durability
2. Length of the distribution channel
3. Amount of handling which the container will receive
4. Variations in climatic conditions which may be encountered between the point of manufacture and sale

Also the following should be taken into consideration:
5. Transportation and storage costs are usually computed on the basis of weight and/or volume and it is clearly in the manufacturer's interest to use packages, which make maximum use of a given space.
6. At the retail level the space/volume factor takes on added importance, as it directly affects the number of different items which can be put on display.

CONSUMER REQUIREMENTS

The packaging of consumer goods was originally a retailing function but competitive pressures and the growth of branding, resulted in the manufacturer assuming responsibility for it. Through the adoption of a distinctive pack and brand name, the manufacturers are able to differentiate their products at the point of sale and to develop advertising and promotional strategies designed to create consumer preference for their products. Further by packaging the product themselves the manufacturers are able to exercise much greater control over the condition in which the ultimate consumer will receive them and so avoid dissatisfaction arising from poor storage and packing at the retailer level.

1. Consumers are receptive to both technical and aesthetic improvements in pack design In many-instances, the satisfaction to be derived from a product is dependent upon its packaging. Many competing products are incapable of differentiation on the basis of objective criteria and in these instances packaging and promotion often constitute the sole distinguishing features upon which the product's success or failure depends.

2. If a manufacturer can offer his or her or she product at a lower price he will be able to increase demand and this is frequently achieved by offering the consumer a variety of different sizes. In addition to catering for variations in household size and usage rates, a range of pack sizes enables the manufacturer to reach consumers with limited purchasing power. The provision of non-standard pack sizes is not only good marketing, it is a socially desirable activity.

3. Many products are not consumed immediately when the package is opened but are used over varying periods of time. To prevent spoilage such products must be packed in reasonable containers, the most familiar of which are the screw-top bottle and jar and the level-lid can. Screw-top jars have long been in use for the packaging of products containing sugar, such as jam, which are susceptible to mould when exposed to the atmosphere.

4. Visual appeal is also an important aspect of pack design, particularly in the case of products of a luxury or semi-luxury nature where the pack itself may add to the image of product quality which the manufacturer is seeking to create.

Some critics have argued that elaborate and expensive packaging is used to:
- Disguise inferior products or
- Permit the seller to inflate the true worth of the product.

Neither claim will sustain much examination, for poor packaging is almost always a good indicator of a poor product and no amount of packaging can disguise a poor product for long. Similarly few consumers are prepared to pay more for a product solely on account of its packaging unless such packaging will add to their enjoyment of the product itself -After

Eight Mints are a classic example - and it is irrelevant if the added satisfaction is purely subjective to the consumer and incapable of objective measurement.

5. Finally, consumers demand packages which satisfy their information needs. Certain information is required by law, e.g. statement of weight and composition of product (although frequently the latter is expressed in language incomprehensible to the average consumer), date of expiry, country of origin etc. In addition to this basic information, consumers favour a clearly marked price (now largely a retailer responsibility), information on how the product should or may be used and, preferably, some view of the contents themselves.

FUTURE TRENDS
In the future we may anticipate greater use of the pack as a competitive weapon.

1. In terms of cost the cheapest form of packaging is the bag in a box, e.g. Kellogg's Cornflakes; next comes the tinplate container, followed, in ascending order, by aluminium, glass, polythene and PVC. Despite their higher cost, increased use is being made of the latter materials because of the added convenience and improved performance that they offer consumers, for which they are clearly prepared to pay.

2. In addition to new improved materials and the developments of containers like the aerosol can and plastic bottle, we may also anticipate a continued increase in the range of products available in packaged form. This trend will be emphasised as more and more women return to work once their children are of school age, which will stimulate the demand for convenience products as well as generating the purchasing power to cover their increased cost.

3. A third trend which has increasing importance is the concern over waste resulting from the packaging materials and protection of the environment. All consumers do not welcome the prodigal waste of resources associated with much of today's non-returnable packaging. This concern is to be seen in the pressure for returnable containers or else the use of materials which may be reused through recycling.

Taken together, these trends predicate that packaging will play an increasingly important role in the marketing mix. At the same time they also suggest that the marketer must be sensitive to the increasing concern for the quality of the environment and the need for conservation of scarce resources when making packaging decisions.

FACTORS TO BE CONSIDERED IN PACKAGE DESIGN

1. **Environmental and Resource Considerations** - litter, disposal and recycling are increasing concerns.
2. **Financial and Cost Factors** - expense of packaging must be justified by increased sales.
3. **Government Regulations** - many EU laws regulate packing and labelling.
4. **Consumer Behaviour and Marketing Strategy Factors** - consumer response to packaging is important. Consumer response can vary between market segments.

The packaging industry sometimes uses an acronym, **VIEW**, in evaluating package designs:
- **VISIBILITY** - does the package stand out from competing packages on the shelf?
- **INFORMATIVE** - does the package indicate at a glance what it contains?
- **EMOTIONAL** - does the package have the right emotional appeal for the product it contains?
- **WORKABLE** - does the package store, protect and serve the product and does it contain the appropriate labelling?

> *In general, Packaging should have the following characteristics:*
> - It must protect what it sells (the product)
> - It must sell what it protects. i.e. It should promote the product by acting as point-of-sale (POS) advertising. Marketers, now with the advent of self-service, think of the package as "the silent salesperson." In addition the package can enhance a product. A change in the package is a relatively inexpensive way to get a "new" product.
> - It must provide functional utility and convenience for the consumer and intermediaries
> - It should enable inspection to occur (where appropriate).
> - It must reflect the needs of the market segment at which it is targeted (e.g. an economy pack for large households).
> - It must reflect consumer and legislative pressure to reduce packaging and use recycled materials.
> - It may be used to stimulate repeat purchases: for example, the sale of re-usable packs and refills increases the likelihood of repurchase.

PACKAGING STRATEGIES
- Packaging the product line
- Changing the package:　　To combat falling sales
　　　　　　　　　　　　　　To attract new customer groups
- Family Packaging: Identical packaging for all products e.g. Heinz
- Reusable Packaging: Stimulates repeat purchases
- Multiple Packaging: Placing several units in 1 pack e.g. 6-can
- Cost-effective packaging
- Ecological Packaging

LABELLING
Another issue in pack design is the use of labelling. Labelling is the part of the product that carries information about the product and the seller. Although much of its use is purely functional - describing the size, weight and contents, providing instruction on how to use or clean the product and meeting health and safety requirements - it also has important promotional aspects.
- First, labelling ensures recognition of the brand. This is particularly important for unpackaged goods such as fruit, which may simply carry stickers.
- Secondly, the use of visibly branded goods by other consumers is an endorsement of the product, so sports wear and carrier bags frequently carry brand names.
- Thirdly, labelling can increase the likelihood that the brand will be reselected when the time comes for repurchase.

MARKETING MANAGEMENT

> TOPIC: PRICING
> LECTURE: 12

PRICING

PRICE is the sum of the values, money or other considerations that consumers exchange for the benefits of having or using a product

Price is that which people have to forego in order to acquire a product or service. To a buyer, price is the value placed on what is exchanged. Something of value - usually purchasing power - is exchanged for satisfaction or utility. Purchasing power depends on a buyer's income, credit, and wealth.

Price is not always money or some other financial consideration. Buyers' concern about price is related to their expectations about the satisfaction or utility associated with a product. Buyers must decide whether the utility gained in an exchange is worth the purchasing power sacrificed.

Price is the only element in the Marketing Mix that produces revenues.

Terms used to describe price

Tuition	Fine	Taxes
Fee	Rent	Wages
Fare	Dues	Interest
Rate	Deposit	Honorarium
Toll	Retainer	Salary
Bribe	Tip	
Commission	Premium	

BARTER - exchanging goods and services for other goods and services rather than for money

VALUE - perceived benefits in relation to price

PRICE COMPETITION - emphasises matching or beating competitors' prices

NON-PRICE COMPETITION - emphasises factors other than price in relation to competitors' products

BEHAVIOURAL ASPECTS OF PRICING.
There is considerable evidence that for many products and services, consumers judge product/service quality by price, a practice which has implications not only for marketing management but for such aspects of economic and social policy as the distribution of income.

Buyer perceptions of price affect the pricing decision. Offered two similar versions of the same product, differing only in price, some consumers choose the most expensive item. Such behaviour may be irrational in terms of economics but is easily explicable in the context of an affluent society in which discretionary income runs at high levels and social status is judged by levels of expenditure and conspicuous consumption.

The gradual extension of the simple marketing concept to the more demanding, broader-based societal marketing concept reflects the marketers' realisation that in future firms will need to take social costs as well as private ones into account.

ECONOMIC ASPECTS OF PRICING

The economist's viewpoint is that the function of the marketplace is to provide a system that automatically ensures the best or 'optimum allocation of resources'. To fulfil this role as the economic problem-solver, the marketer has to be sensitive to changes in customer needs and wants, and responsive to any changes in the conditions of the market, demand or supply. Price is the critical variable in this mechanism.

Changes in customer demand cause price to change. Price changes signal changing profitability to suppliers, causing them to reassess their output decisions. This central and dynamic role of price causes economists to describe price as the invisible hand, which works to bring demand and supply together. The economic role of price is to allocate products and match them to market opportunities that develop from increased or decreased demand.

SETTING PRICES

Despite the increased role of non-price factors in the modern marketing process, price remains an important element in the marketing mix. Many internal and external factors influence the company's pricing decision.

Setting prices is not easy. It involves making a number of guesses about the future. In an ideal situation, an organisation should proceed as follows:

1. Identify the target market segment for the product or service, and decide what share of it is desired and how quickly.
2. Establish the price range that would be acceptable to occupants of this segment. If this looks unpromising, it is still possible that consumers might be educated to accept higher price levels, though this may take time.
3. Examine the prices (and costs if possible) of potential or actual competitors.
4. Examine the range of possible prices within different combinations of the marketing mix (e.g. different levels of product quality or distribution methods).
5. Determine whether the product can be sold profitably at each price based upon anticipated sales levels (i.e. by calculating break-even point) and if so, whether these profits will meet strategic objectives for profitability.
6. If only a modest profit is expected it may be below the threshold figure demanded by an organisation for all its activities. In these circumstances, it may be necessary to modify product specifications downwards until costs are reduced sufficiently to produce the desired profit.
7. Anticipate the likely reaction of competitors (actual or potential).

INTERNAL FACTORS AFFECTING PRICE

Internal factors affecting price include marketing objectives, costs and organisational considerations.

1. MARKETING OBJECTIVES.

Price is only one of the marketing-mix tools that the company uses to achieve its marketing objectives. Price decisions must be co-ordinated with product design, distribution, and promotion decisions to form a consistent and effective marketing programme.

Before setting price, the company must decide on its strategy for the product. If the company has selected its target market and positioning carefully, then its marketing-mix strategy, including price, will be fairly straightforward. Pricing strategy is largely determined by past decisions on market positioning. However, the organisation may be seeking additional objectives such as survival, current profit maximisation, market-share maximisation, or product-quality leadership.

- Survival can be the primary factor in setting price especially in marginal businesses or industries.
- Current Profit Maximisation means the company is emphasising short-term results over long-run performance.
- Market-Share Leadership affects price when the company seeks the dominant market share.
- Product-Quality Leadership tends to push prices high. This pricing strategy may be linked to niching strategy in other discussions.
- Other Objectives include pricing low to keep out potential competitors, support resellers, or to prevent government intervention. Non-profit organisations sometimes practice partial cost recover or social pricing.

2. COSTS.

Demand largely sets a ceiling to the price that a company can charge for its products, and company costs set the floor. The company wants to charge a price that covers all of its costs of producing, distributing, and selling the product, including a fair return for its effort and risk. A company's costs take two forms, fixed and variable costs.

- **Fixed costs** are costs that do not vary with production or sales revenue.
- **Variable costs** are usually constant per unit.
- **Total costs** are the sum of the two.

Management wants to charge a price that will at least cover the total production costs at a given level of production. It should be noted that:

- Costs vary at Different Levels of Production.
- Costs can be spread out over more units but reach diminishing returns at some point.
- Costs may be a Function of Production Experience. The learning curve concept notes that experience making the product usually leads to lower costs.

3. ORGANISATIONAL CONSIDERATIONS.

Management must decide who within the organisation will be responsible for setting the price. In large organisations top management will usually set overall pricing policies and determine pricing objectives, with pricing itself left to divisional or line managers. In smaller organisations top management may set prices.

Various people (such as sales managers, production managers, finance managers, and accountants) within the organisation may be involved in pricing decisions.

EXTERNAL FACTORS AFFECTING PRICE

External factors affecting price include market and demand, competitor prices and offers, and economic conditions.

1. MARKET AND DEMAND.

Each price that the company might charge will lead to a different level of demand and therefore have a different effect on its marketing objectives.

a. Pricing in Different Types of Markets

- Pure Competition - is characterised by many buyers and sellers so that no one agent affects pricing. Going rate pricing is the rule.
- Monopolistic Competition - consists of many buyers and sellers trading over a range of prices. Products can be differentiated in quality, features, or styles.
- Oligopolistic Competition - consists of few sellers each sensitive to the other's pricing and marketing strategies. Barriers to entry prohibit new sellers from entering the market.
- Pure Monopoly - consists of a single seller. The seller may by a government, a private regulated monopoly, or an unregulated monopoly. Pricing may be linked to other than cost or profit factors, including fear of competition entering or regulation.

b. Consumer Perceptions of Price and Value.

Buyers ultimately decide prices. Marketers must combine technical expertise with creative judgement and an awareness of buyers' motivations.

c. Analysing the Price-Demand Relationship.

The demand curve shows the number of units the market will buy in a given time period at various prices.

d. Price elasticity of Demand.

Marketers must know how responsive demand would be to a change in price, i.e. they need to know the price elasticity of demand.

- If demand hardly changes with a small change in price, demand is inelastic.
- If a small change in prices changes demand greatly, demand is elastic.

Price elasticity of demand is defined as the percentage change in quantity demanded, divided by the percentage change in price; it is usually a minus figure as demand is expected to fall with an increase in price.

2. COMPETITORS PRICES AND OFFERS.

While market demand might set a ceiling and costs set a floor to pricing, competitors' prices and possible price reactions help the firm establish where its prices may be set. The company needs to learn the price and quality of each competitor's offer.
This can be done in several ways:

- The firm can send out comparison shoppers to price and compare competitor's offers.
- The firm can acquire competitors' price lists and buy competitors' equipment and take it apart.
- The firm can ask buyers how they perceive the price and quality of each competitor's offer.

Once the company is aware of competitor's prices and offers, it can use them as an orienting point for its own pricing. Some companies have standing policies to match price changes of their competition. Other respond with non-price changes in the marketing mix such as increased features or performance.

3. ECONOMIC CONDITIONS.
Economic conditions can have a strong impact on the firm's pricing strategies. Economic factors such as inflation, boom or recession, and interest rates affect pricing decisions because they affect both the costs of producing a product and consumers perceptions of the product's price and value.

4. OTHER ENVIRONMENTAL FACTORS
which may include:
- The role of resellers in the channel of distribution may affect pricing.
- Government's role can also be a consideration
- Social concerns.

PRICING APPROACHES
The price the company charges will be somewhere between one that is too low to produce any profit and one that is too high to produce any demand. The company must consider competitors' prices and other external and internal factors to find the best price between these two extremes. Three approaches that the company may use are a cost-based approach, a buyer-based approach, and a competition based approach.

1. Cost-based approaches.
    a. Cost-plus pricing
    b. Break even analysis and target profit pricing

In cost-plus pricing, a standard mark-up is added to the cost of the product.
In break even analysis and target profit pricing, the firm tries to determine the price at which it will break even or make the target profit it is seeking.

Advantages of a cost based approach to pricing
- Managers usually feel more certain about costs than about what customers will pay
- Prices are easier to justify in terms of costs rather than benefits
- A cost-based approach to pricing is administratively easier than judging market-based issues
- Prices based on cost appear socially more acceptable and are less open to accusations of exploitation
- A cost-plus approach should ensure that an organisation remains profitable.

Disadvantages of a cost based approach to pricing
- Costs are not always easy to identify
- It ignores the way customers use price
- It ignores the relative value of an offering compared with competitors
- Costs will often vary with volume
- Market objectives are not usually related to costs
- Costings between products is highly dependent on the way costs are allocated In the end, the consumer decides whether the company has set the right price. The consumer weighs the price against the perceived value of using the product. If the price exceeds the sum of the value, consumers will not buy the product.

2. Buyer-based approach.
Perceived-value pricing uses buyers perceptions of value, not the seller's cost, as the key to pricing. The company uses the non-price variables in the marketing-mix to build up perceived value in buyers' minds.

3. Competition-based approach.
   a. Going-rate pricing
   b. Sealed-bid pricing

In going-rate pricing, the firm bases its price largely on competitors' prices, with less attention paid to its own costs or to demand. The firm might charge the same, more, or less than its major competitors.

In sealed-bid pricing, firms bid for jobs, with the firms basing the price on what it thinks other firms will be bidding rather than on its own costs or demand.

PRICING STRATEGIES

1. PRICING INNOVATIVE NEW PRODUCTS (new to the world)

a. Price Skimming Market skimming pricing is the strategy of setting high initial prices to skim maximum profits from each successive layer of the target market. Skimming strategies typically set a price as high as some segments will bear. Once all customers within this segment have purchased, prices are lowered only so far as the next segment needs to be persuaded to buy. Innovative new products have very little or no direct competition. Moreover "innovators" and "early adopters" (from 'diffusion of innovation") are usually willing to pay more for owning a unique new product. Marketers charge a high price (to "skim the cream of the market" off the top) initially in hopes of recouping development costs early. As competition increases, prices drop.

b. Penetration Pricing The opposite of skimming, marketers charge a very low price for the new product on hopes of drawing as many people to it as possible, and establishing their brand in consumers' minds before competition begins. This strategy is appropriate when a quick competitive response to the new product is expected.

2. PRICING IMITATIVE NEW PRODUCTS

Pricing imitative new products depends on the particulars of the situation, especially the competition. Since the product is not "new to the world," less latitude exists in developing a pricing policy.

3. OTHER PRICING STRATEGIES

a. Product Line Pricing - In product line pricing, management must decide on the price steps to set between each product in the line. Companies often use price points to target distinctive combinations of product features and value represented by a particular price.

b. Optional Product Pricing - Charging separately for each option or feature the consumer requests. This requires that features not be bundled together as standard equipment, but offered separately, and charged for separately.

c. Product Bundle Pricing - An opposite approach to optional product pricing. Several features, attributes or services are included at one price, whether the consumer uses them or not.

d. Captive Pricing - Products that serve as supplies or compliments to other goods may be sold at a premium price, particularly when
- there is little competition
- the supplies or compliments work only for one brand of product, making substitutes unavailable.

e. **Loss Leader-Pricing** - Cut price on a popular item to draw consumers to the store in hopes they will buy other, more profitable products while there.

f. **By-Product Pricing** - Waste from production and distribution may be marketable as by-products.

PRICE-ADJUSTMENT STRATEGIES

a. **Discount Pricing and Allowances**
- **Cash Discounts** are price reductions to buyers who pay bills promptly. They are made from the face amount of the invoice after the trade and quantity discounts from the list price.

2 elements are present in the cash discount:
  a. The % discount itself and
  b. The time period in which the invoice must be paid
      2/10, n 30, means 2% discount if paid within 10 days and no discount in 30 days
      2/10 eom means 10 days after the end of the month
      2/10, extra 30, extends discount for 30 days.

A retailer should always take advantage of cash discounts. It is cheaper to borrow from the Bank than to "borrow" from a vendor.

- **Quantity Discounts** refer to price reductions per unit on large volumes. They are granted because it is more economical for the vendor to sell a product in larger units. The seller's costs associated with shipping, delivery, salesman's costs, billing and collection are reduced when large orders are filled.

- **Trade or Functional Discounts** are granted to channel members who perform various marketing functions. These include buying, selling, storage, financing, risk bearing or taking title, bulk-breaking units into smaller or single items, transporting and disseminating market information.

- **Seasonal Discounts** are granted to buyers who purchase merchandise out of season. They are used by vendors to encourage buyers to place orders early in the season. In effect the vendor is shifting the marketing functions of storage and warehousing to the buyer. The seasonal discount is the incentive to the retailer to do so. The vendor is also benefiting by making better use of his production facilities.

- **Promotional discounts and Allowances** such as trade-ins for turning in old items on new purchases or promotional allowances for participating in seller sponsored advertising can also lower buyer prices. They are granted in partial payment for advertising and promotional services performed by the retailer e.g.
  - 25-cent-per-case allowance
  - 12 + 1 (one free for every dozen)
  - Point-of-Sale display materials
  - Money amounts for specific advertising purposes.
  - Dealer sales contests
  - Co-operative advertising
  - Speciality advertising items-pens, memopads, ashtrays etc.

b. Discriminatory Pricing - Discriminatory pricing refers to pricing differences not based on cost and takes several forms:
- Customer-segment pricing, such as senior citizen discounts.
- Product-form pricing varies costs on versions of a product by features but not production costs.
- Location pricing stems from preferences such as seating in a theatre.
- Time pricing refers to price breaks given at times of lower demand.

c. Psychological Pricing - A key component in psychological pricing is the reference price consumers carry in their mind when considering sellers prices.

d. Promotional Pricing - Promotional prices are temporary reductions used to attract customers. Loss leaders may be offered below costs to attract attention to an entire line.

e. Value Pricing - This strategy offers a desired combination of features and prices to identified target markets.

f. Geographical Pricing
- FOB-Origin Pricing - Free On Board has customer pay freight.
- Uniform Delivered Pricing - The company charges the same price to all.
- Zone Pricing - Different areas pay different prices on freight but all customers within the same area pay the same freight charges.
- Basing-Point Pricing - All customers charged freight from a specified billing location.
- Freight-Absorption Pricing - The seller pays all shipping costs to get the desired business.
- International Pricing - Firms may charge the same price throughout the world, especially for high-ticket, high-tech products like jetliners. Or it may offer different prices based upon differing taxes, tariffs, distribution, and promotion costs.

PRICING STRATEGIES BASED ON PRODUCT QUALITY/PRICE COMBINATIONS

PRICE

PRODUCT QUALITY	LOW	MEDIUM	HIGH
LOW	CHEAP-VALUE STRATEGY	OUT-OF-STEP STRATEGY	RIP-OFF STRATEGY
MEDIUM	GOOD VALUE STRATEGY	MIDDLE-OF-THE-ROAD STRATEGY	OVERCHARGING STRATEGY
HIGH	SUPERB VALUE STRATEGY	HIGH-VALUE STRATEGY	PREMIUM STRATEGY

PRICING STRATEGY DEVELOPMENT PROCESS
Example of pricing development

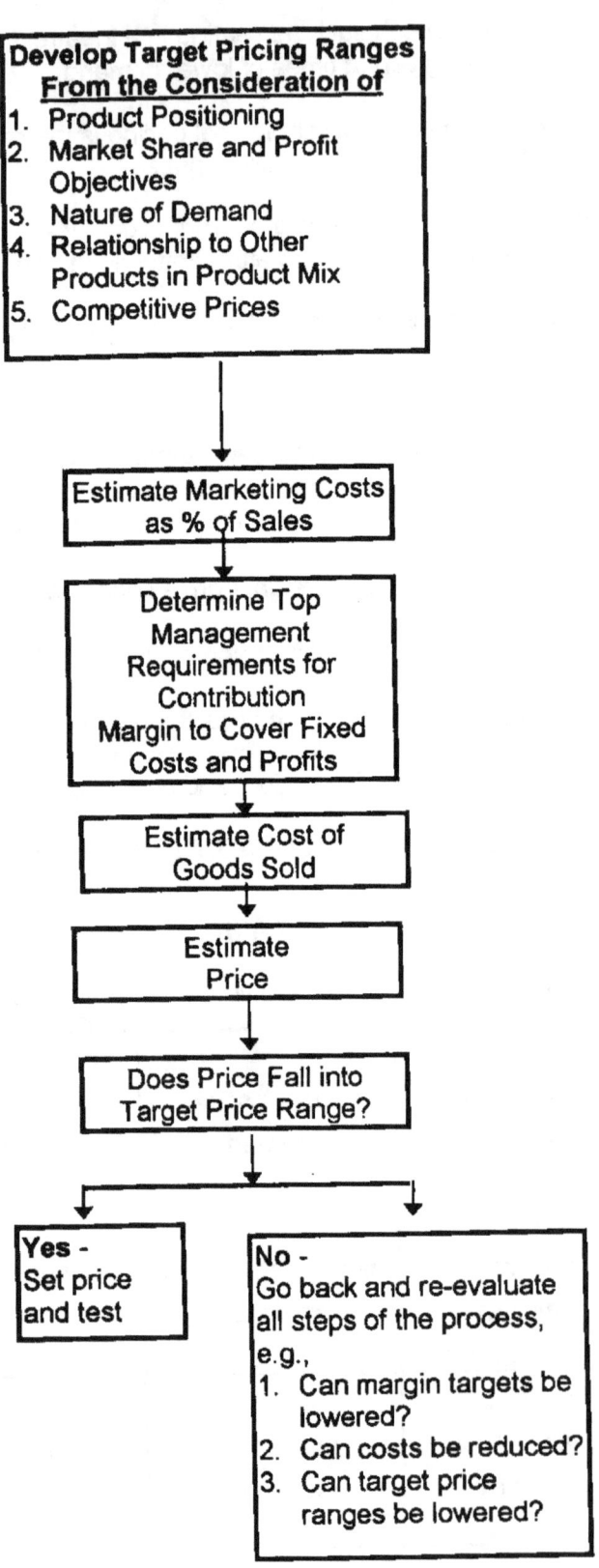

MARKETING MANAGEMENT

TOPIC: DISTRIBUTION
LECTURE: *13*

DISTRIBUTION

Producing products that customers want, pricing them correctly and developing well-designed promotional plans are necessary but not sufficient conditions for customer satisfaction. The final part of the marketing mix is distribution, the 'Place' element. Products need to be available in adequate quantities, in convenient locations and at times when customers want to buy them. Producers need to consider not only the needs of their ultimate customer but also the requirement of channel intermediaries, those organisations who facilitate the distribution of products to customers.

Distribution is the process by means of which goods or services are made available and accessible to consumers.

The principal concerns for marketing people in establishing the ground rules for a distribution network should be:
- Timing - will the product be available when the market expects it?
- Location - will it be in the places where consumers expect to find it?
- Reliability - will the distribution system deliver what is required of it or will stockists be telling consumers 'Sorry, we're still waiting for another delivery'?

Efficient distribution should be an important organisational objective. Having made a decision to purchase, the consumer will then want the product as soon as possible and a good distribution system will 'take the waiting out of wanting'.

It is not enough that a distribution system should be adequate; exceptional distribution will provide an organisation with a significant market advantage.
In addition to securing the correct strategic solutions to distribution, it is also important to ensure that the process is efficient. Examples of late, damaged, incorrect or wastefully small deliveries, of vast stockpiles of unsold products and of raw materials or finished goods simply going missing are manifestations of a lack of management concern with the process.

As a result of these problems, many organisations now implement physical distribution management (PDM) systems. PDM is concerned with the design and operation of efficient systems for the inward movement of raw materials to the point of manufacture and for the outward movement of finished goods to the consumer.

The Significance of Physical Distribution and Logistics Management

- **Physical Distribution** is organising the movement and storage of a finished product to the customer.

- **Logistics management** is organising the cost-effective flow of raw materials, in-process inventory, finished goods and related information from point of origin to consumption.

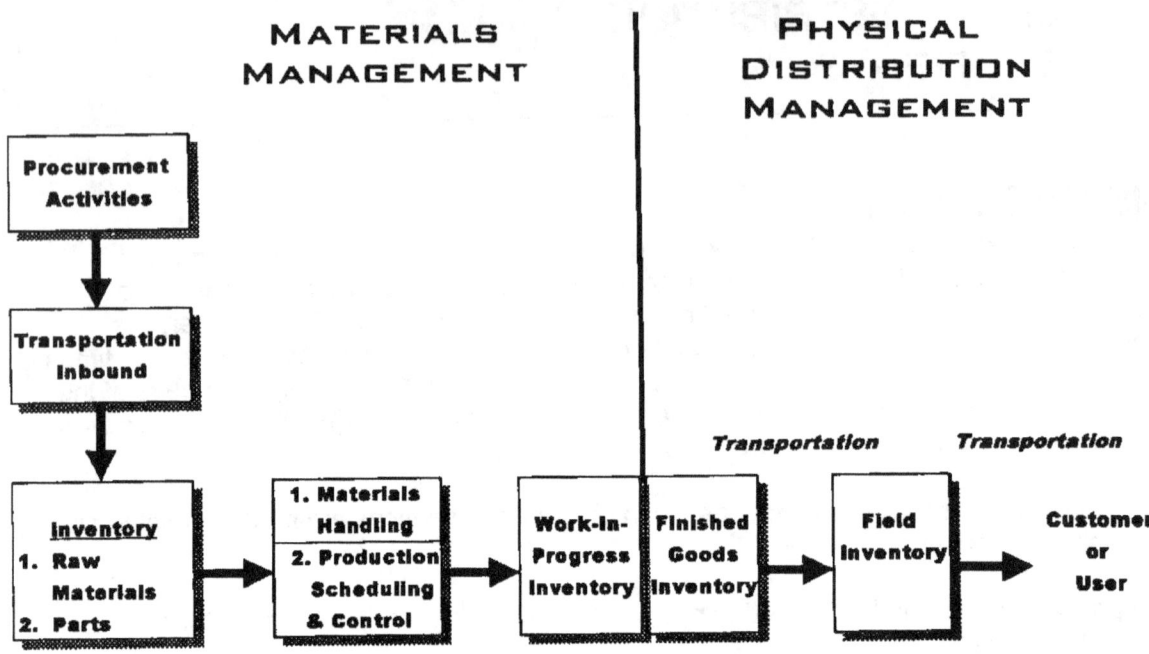

THE NATURE OF MARKETING CHANNELS

The distribution component of the marketing mix focuses on the decisions and actions involved in making products available to consumers when and where they want to purchase them. Channel decisions are critical because they determine a product's market presence and buyers' accessibility to the product

Distribution involves the use of one or more channels to facilitate transactions between supplier and consumers.

A channel is the route along which pass one or more of the following:
- the product or service itself
- the title to the goods (i.e. ownership)
- payment
- promotional materials
- consumer feedback

A marketing channel (or channel of distribution) is a group of individuals and organisations that directs the flow of products from producers to customers. Providing customer benefits should be the driving force behind all marketing channel activities.

A marketing intermediary (middleman) links producers to other middlemen or to ultimate product users through contractual arrangements or through the purchase and resale of products.
1. Wholesalers buy and resell products to other wholesalers, to retailers and to industrial customers.
2. Retailers purchase products and resell them to ultimate consumers.

Marketing channels create utility i.e.
- **Time** utility is having products available when customers want them.
- **Place** utility is having products available where customers want to purchase them.
- **Possession** utility provides the customer with access to the product to use or to store for future use.

Marketing channels facilitate exchange efficiencies.
- Marketing intermediaries can reduce the cost of exchanges by performing certain services or functions.
- Eliminating wholesalers would not do away with the need for the services they provide.

Why are marketing intermediaries used?
- Producers lack financial resources
- Specialisation and economies of scale
- Superior efficiency in making goods widely available and accessible to target markets
- Bridge the gap between assortment desired by the market and production/transportation efficiencies
- Transactional efficiency
- Contactual efficiency

TYPES OF MARKETING CHANNELS

CHANNELS FOR CONSUMER PRODUCTS
Channel level - Each supplier that performs work in bringing the product and/or its title closer to the final buyer

1. Producer to consumer is a direct channel that includes customers who harvest their own fruit from commercial growers or buy goods directly from factories.

> **Zero-level channel** - No intermediaries (direct marketing)
>
> Manufacturer
> |
> Consumer

2. The producer-to-retailer-to-consumer channel is used by large retailers that buy in large quantities from manufacturers.

> **One-level channel** - One intermediary
>
> Manufacturer
> |
> Retailer
> |
> Consumer

3. The producer-to-wholesaler-to-retailer-to-consumer channel is a practical option for a producer that sells to hundreds of thousands of consumers through thousands of retailers, such as producers of convenience goods.

Two-level channel

Manufacturer
|
Wholesaler
|
Retailer
|
Consumer

4. The producer-to-agent-to-wholesaler-to-retailer-to-consumer channel is used for products intended for mass distribution.

Three-level channel

Manufacturer
|
Agent
|
Wholesaler
|
Retailer
|
Consumer

Examples of Distribution Channels for Consumer Goods

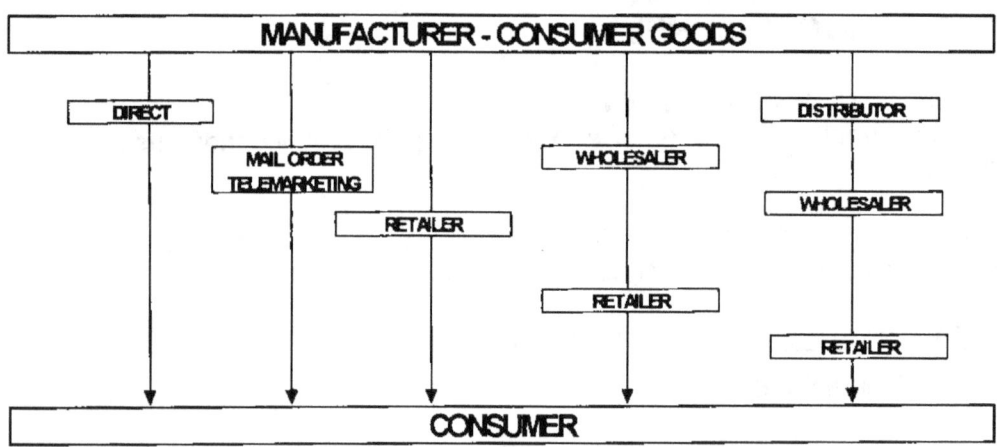

CHANNELS FOR INDUSTRIAL PRODUCTS

1. The producer-to-industrial-buyer channel is necessary for many manufacturers of industrial goods because industrial buyers often prefer to communicate directly with the producer, especially for expensive or technically complex products.
2. Producers and industrial buyers may be linked by an industrial distributor, an independent business organisation that takes title to products and carries inventories for resale to industrial buyers.
3. Producers and industrial buyers may be linked by a manufacturers' agent or representative, an independent businessperson who sells complementary products of several producers in assigned territories and is compensated through commissions.
4. The channel may include both a manufacturer's agent and an industrial distributor between the producer and industrial customer.

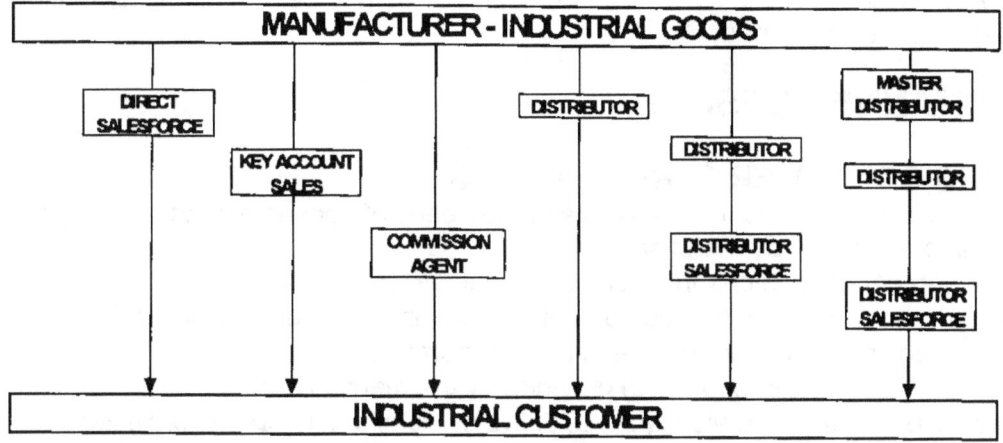

Multiple marketing channels and channel alliances

1. Manufacturers may use several marketing channels simultaneously to reach diverse target markets.
2. Dual distribution is the use of two or more marketing channels for distributing the same products to the same target market.
3. A strategic channel alliance exists when the products of one organisation are distributed through the marketing channels of another organisation.

FUNCTIONS PERFORMED BY CHANNELS

- **Information** This function involves gathering and distributing marketing research and intelligence about the environment for planning purposes.
- **Promotion** This involves developing and spreading persuasive communications about an offer.
- **Contact** - involves finding and communicating with prospective buyers.
- **Matching** This function consists of shaping and fitting the offer to the buyer's needs by manufacturing, grading, assembling and packaging.
- **Negotiation** This involves reaching an agreement on price and other terms.
- **Ordering**
- **Financing** This function addresses the acquiring and using of funds to cover the costs of channel work.
- **Risk Taking** This function assumes the risk of carrying out the channel work.
- **Physical Possession** This function consists of the transporting and storing of goods.
- **Payment**
- **Title** - ownership

DISTRIBUTION CHANNEL DECISIONS

Distribution channel decisions are among the most complex and challenging decisions facing a firm. Each channel system creates a different level of sales and costs. Once a distribution channel has been chosen, the firm must usually stick with it for a long time. The chosen channel strongly affects and is affected by, the other elements in the marketing mix. Each firm needs to identify alternative ways to reach its market. Available means vary from direct selling to using one, two, three or more intermediary channel levels. Channel design begins with assessing customer channel-service needs and company channel objectives and constraints. The company then identifies the major channel alternatives in terms of the types of intermediaries, the number of intermediaries and the channel responsibilities of each.

STEPS IN CHANNEL DESIGN

1. ANALYSING CONSUMER SERVICE NEEDS

Channel design decisions begin with an analysis of the needs of consumers in target market segments to be served by the channel:
- Lot size - Number of units channel permits typical customer to buy
- Waiting time - Average time that customers of a channel wait for receipt goods
- Spatial convenience - Customer ease in product purchase
- Product variety - Assortment breadth provided by the marketing channel
- Service backup - Add on services (credit, delivery, installation, repairs) provided by the channel

2. SETTING THE CHANNEL OBJECTIVES AND CONSTRAINTS

Channel objectives must specify product characteristics, company characteristics, middlemen characteristics and consider both the competitors' channels and environmental factors.

Establishing channel objectives:
- State targeted service output levels
- Minimise total channel costs

3. IDENTIFYING MAJOR ALTERNATIVES

a. TYPES OF MIDDLEMEN
- **Company Salesforce.** This approach expands the company's presence in the market by assigning its own people territories to sell the products.
- **Manufacturer's Agency.** This approach hires independent firms whose salesforce markets related products from many companies. Agents seeking to best satisfy their customers can honestly represent each product well.
- **Industrial Distributors.** This approach contracts with existing distributors in different regions who will buy and resell a product line

b. NUMBER OF MIDDLEMEN
Intensity of market coverage refers to the number and kinds of outlets in which a product is sold. The choice depends on the characteristics of the product and the target market.
- **Intensive Distribution** - utilises as many outlets as possible and is especially appropriate for convenience goods and common raw materials.
- **Selective Distribution** - uses more than one outlet per market but less than all available outlets. This strategy gains good market coverage and gains better than average selling effort. It is appropriate for shopping products, such as stereos.
- **Exclusive distribution**, using only one outlet in a large area to distribute a product, is suitable for products purchased infrequently, consumed over a long period of time or requiring service or information to fit buyers' needs, such as expensive imported sports cars. This strategy is appropriate for many high prestige goods. Distributor selling effort is usually very strong.

Distribution Method	Product Type	Brand
EXCLUSIVE SELECTIVE INTENSIVE	Specialty Goods Shopping Goods Convenience Goods	PORSCHE SONY BIC

c. TERMS AND RESPONSIBILITIES OF CHANNEL MEMBERS
Responsibilities of Channel Members
Channel members need to agree on price policies, conditions of sale, territory rights and the specific services to be performed by each party.
- Price policy - Producer establishes list price and discounts
- Conditions of sale - Payment terms and producer guarantees
- Distributors' territorial rights
- Mutual services and responsibilities

4. EVALUATING THE MAJOR ALTERNATIVES
- **Economic Criteria** consider the different levels of sales and costs for each alternative.
- **Control Criteria** must weigh the needs for directing the channel against the benefits of using outside businesses. The supplier usually seeks to maximise control.
- **Adaptive Criteria** consider the benefits of each alternative against the loss of flexibility of long-term contracts. Suppliers seek channels that can swiftly change to the needs of the marketplace

5. SELECT CHANNEL
CHANNEL MANAGEMENT DECISIONS

1. SELECTING CHANNEL MEMBERS
Producers vary in their ability to attract qualified middlemen. When selecting middlemen the company should determine the characteristics of the better middlemen available.

2. MOTIVATING CHANNEL MEMBERS
Channel members must be motivated to perform.
- Positive motivators come from high margins, distribution programming, special deals, premiums, co-operative advertising allowances, display allowances, merchandising programs desired by distributors and sales contests.
- Negative motivators may include threatening margins, delaying delivery or ending the relationship.

3. EVALUATING CHANNEL MEMBERS
Assessing channel members requires regular measurement of performance against established criteria such as sales quotas, inventory levels, customer delivery time, training and overall customer service for each channel member.

4. CHANNEL MODIFICATION
- Add or drop individual channel members
- Add or drop particular market channels
- Develop a totally new way to sell goods in all markets

THE PERFECT MIDDLEMAN
- Has access to the market that the manufacturer wants to reach.
- Carries adequate stocks of the manufacturer's products and a satisfactory assortment of other products.
- Has an effective promotional program - advertising, personal selling and product displays. Promotional demands placed on the manufacturer are in line with what the manufacturer intends to do.
- Provides services to customers - credit, delivery, installation and product repair - and honours the product warranty conditions.
- Pays its bills on time and has capable management

THE PERFECT MANUFACTURER
- Provides a desirable assortment of products - well designed, properly priced, attractively packaged and delivered on time and in adequate quantities.
- Builds product demand for these products by advertising them.
- Furnishes promotional assistance to its middlemen.
- Provides managerial assistance for its middlemen.
- Honours product warranties and provides repair and installation service.

THE PERFECT COMBINATION
Probably doesn't exist.

MARKETING MANAGEMENT

TOPIC: PROMOTION
LECTURE: *14*

PROMOTION

Promotion is one of the four major elements of the company's marketing mix. The main promotion tools are:
- **Advertising**
- **Sales Promotion**
- **Public Relations**
- **Personal Selling**
- **Direct Marketing**

All the elements of the Promotion Mix work together to achieve the company's communication objectives.

THE ROLE OF PROMOTION

Promotion's role is to communicate with individuals, groups or organisations to directly or indirectly facilitate exchanges by informing and persuading one or more of the audiences to accept an organisation's products.

To facilitate exchanges directly, marketers communicate with selected audiences about their companies and their goods, services and ideas. Marketers indirectly facilitate exchanges by focusing information about company activities and products on interest groups, current and potential investors, regulatory agencies and society in general.

Promotion can play a comprehensive communication role. Some promotional activities can be directed towards helping a company justify its existence and maintain healthy, positive relationships between itself and various groups in the marketing environment. To develop and implement effective promotional activities, a firm must use information from the marketing environment, often obtained from its marketing information system. The degree to which marketers can effectively use promotion to maintain positive relationships with environmental forces depends largely on the quantity and quality of information an organisation takes in.

A Basic Communications Model

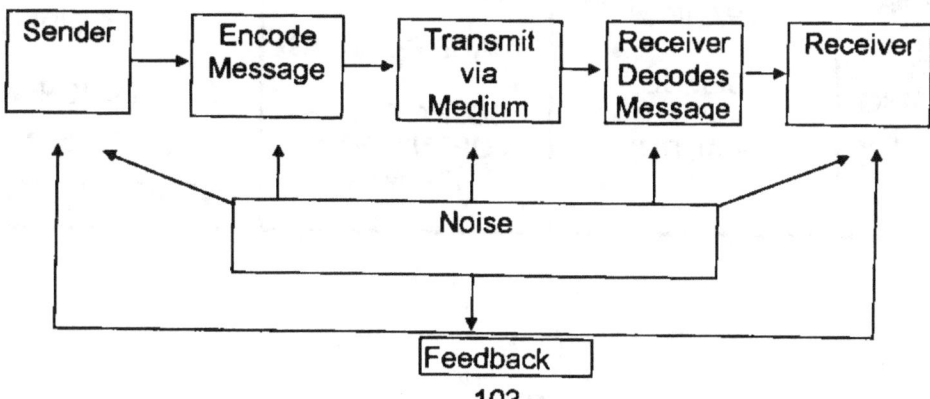

SETTING THE PROMOTION MIX

Strategic decisions must be made on how to allocate the budget to each of the promotion tools. Typically setting the mix is a function of the objectives of the campaign and the nature of each of the promotion tools available.

THE PROMOTION MIX

ADVERTISING	PERSONAL SELLING	PUBLIC RELATIONS	SALES PROMOTION
TV	SALES FORCE	PUBLIC RELATIONS	EXHIBITIONS
RADIO	SERVICE FORCE	TRADE RELATIONS	PACKAGING
GENERAL PRESS	RECEPTIONIST		REUSABLE CONTAINERS
SPECIALISED PRESS	SWITCHBOARD OPERATOR	PRESS RELATIONS	SPECIAL OFFERS
			FREE SAMPLES
DIRECT MAIL	HIGH LEVEL CONTACTS	EMPLOYEE RELATIONS	COMPETITIONS
			COUPONS
POSTERS	TECHNICAL COMMUNICATION	PUBLICITY - "FREE ADVERTISING"	2 For The Price Of 1
			12 + 1
NEON SIGNS BANNERS	WOM (Word Of Mouth)	PRESS RELEASE	PERSONALITY PROMOTIONS
			"Give Aways"
AIRSHIPS	TELEPHONE SELLING	SPONSORSHIP	BAGS
HOTEL & AIRPORT LOUNGES	RECIPROCAL TRADING	SYMPOSIUM	SALES LITERATURE
		SEMINAR	CATALOGUES & PRICE LISTS
ELECTRONIC MEDIA	EDUCATIONAL CAMPAIGNS	COCKTAILS	CALENDARS & DIARIES
INTERNET	LOAN EQUIPMENT	CO. EXECUTIVES SPEECHES CLUBS	HOUSE JOURNALS
			SHOWROOMS
TELEMEDIA	TRADE-IN	IMAGE BUILDING	FILMS & VIDEO
DIRECT ADVERTISING & MARKETING	DEMOS	CO. PARTIES & OPEN DOOR EVENTS	CO. STATIONERY
	TRIAL RUN		UNIFORMS
			VEHICLE LIVERY

THE NATURE OF EACH PROMOTION TOOL

1. Advertising. Advertising's public nature helps legitimise the product. It also allows marketers to repeat the message to a wide audience. Large-scale campaigns communicate something positive about the seller's size, popularity and success.

2. Personal Selling. Personal selling is the most effective promotion tool at certain stages in the buying process, especially in building preferences, convictions and actions. The personal contact is two-way and allows adaptation to buyer reactions and the establishment of relationships.

3. Sales Promotion. Sales promotion includes coupons, contests, cents-off deals, premiums, rebates and other techniques designed to elicit a quick response. Sales promotions usually influence the timing of a purchase rather than the decision to purchase.

4. Public Relations. Public relations includes news stories, features and reporting on company activities from objective and credible third-party sources. These events are perceived as more believable than company-controlled promotions.

5. Direct marketing Direct marketing includes Mailings, Fax-mail, E-mail, Voice-mail, Electronic shopping, TV shopping, Catalogues, Telemarketing,
Characteristics of direct marketing:
- Non-public - directed to a specific person
- Customised - to appeal to the addressed individual
- Up to date - a message can be prepared very quickly for delivery to an individual
- Interactive - the message can be altered depending on the person's response

FACTORS IN SETTING THE PROMOTION MIX
Marketers vary the compositions of promotional mixes for many reasons. An organisation's promotional mix (or mixes) is not an unchanging part of the marketing mix. The specific promotional mix ingredients used and the intensity with which an organisation uses them depend on the organisation's promotional resources, objectives and policies and a variety of factors such as:

1. Type of Product/Market.
The characteristics of the product influence the promotional mix ingredients. Advertising weighs heavily in consumer markets whereas personal selling plays the greatest role in industrial markets. The size, geographic distribution and socio-economic characteristics of an organisation's target market also help dictate the ingredients to be included in a product's promotional mix.

2. Push versus Pull Strategy.
Push strategies rely on personal selling and sales promotions to encourage intermediaries to take the product. Pull strategies rely on advertising and consumer promotions to build up demand in the target market of ultimate consumer whose behaviour effectively "pulls" the product through the channel.

3. Buyer Readiness State.
Advertising and public relations help create awareness and increase knowledge. Liking and preference are more affected by personal selling and advertising together. Conviction and purchase come first from advertising and then personal selling to close depending upon the kind of product being considered.

4. Product Life Cycle Stage.
The stage in the product life cycle also describes different appropriate promotion mix variations. Introduction utilises advertising and public relations to build awareness and personal selling to facilitate motivate channel members to carry it. In growth, the need for personal selling diminishes. In maturity, personal selling helps differentiate it again in distribution. In decline, sales promotion may be the most emphasised of the promotion mix tools.

5. Cost and availability.
The costs of promotional methods and the availability of promotional techniques are major factors to analyse when developing a promotional mix.

STEPS IN DEVELOPING EFFECTIVE COMMUNICATION

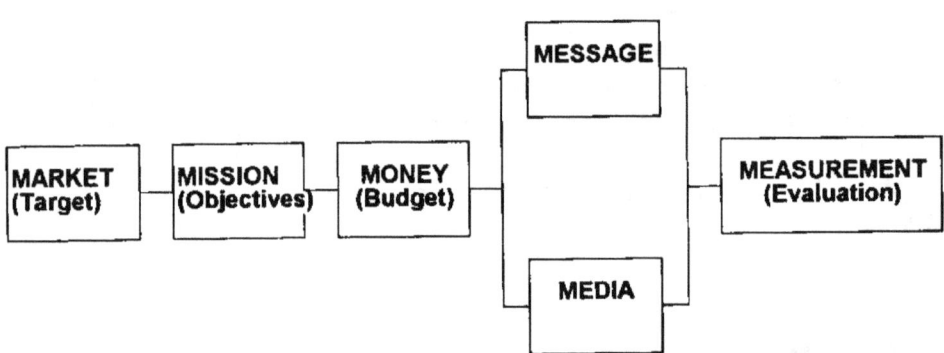

Kotler's 6Ms - Major Decisions in Advertising

A. IDENTIFYING THE TARGET AUDIENCE
The target audience will heavily affect the communicator's decisions on what will be said, how it will be said, when it will be said, where it will be said and who will say it.

B. SETTING THE OBJECTIVES - DETERMINING THE RESPONSE SOUGHT
Responses correspond to buyer readiness states.
    1. Awareness. Marketers must first establish in the customer an awareness that the product exists.
    2. Knowledge. After awareness, the marketing communicator seeks to provide knowledge about the product's benefits and link these to the consumer's needs.
    3. Liking. Marketers must link information to positive affect so that consumers feel good about the product.

4. Preference. Marketers attempt to turn liking into preference so that the product will achieve hierarchical superiority over other competing and also liked products.

5. Conviction. In this state marketers help encourage consumers that product use is a necessary action step to satisfy a demand for the product's benefits.

6. Purchase. Many target consumers may still need encouragement from additional promotions to actually make the purchase.

C. SETTING THE TOTAL PROMOTION BUDGET

1. **Affordable Method.** This method involves setting a promotion budget based upon what management thinks the company can afford.

2. **Percentage-of-Sales Method.** This method sets promotion budgets at a certain percentage of current or projected sales or price of the product.

3. **Competitive-Parity Method.** This method sets promotion budgets in line with what the competition spends on promotion.

4. **Objective-and-Task Method.** This method sets budgets by defining specific objectives, determining what tasks are necessary to meet them, estimates the cost of performing the tasks and sets the promotion budget according to the estimates.

D. CHOOSING A MESSAGE

1. Message Content.

- Rational appeals relate to the audience's self-interest. Rational appeals are grounded in objective, logical reasons for purchasing a product such as improved performance, increased quality, better reliability and increased productivity.
- Emotional appeals attempt to elicit either positive or negative feelings that will facilitate a purchase.
- Moral appeals are directed to the consumer's sense of right and wrong and are often used in conjunction with the marketing of social causes.

2. Message Structure.

Marketers deal with three message structure issues.

- First, marketers must decide whether or not to draw a conclusion in the message or let the audience draw their own.
- Second, marketers must decide on the type of argument to be used.
    - One-sided arguments work best when the audience is unlikely to examine the information critically.
    - Two-sided arguments are useful if the audience is likely to be exposed to other information not under control of the marketer that may refute some of the product claims.
- Third, argument order must be decided.

3. Message Format.

Format issues involve sensory qualities, colour in visual ads, sound in radio and effective use of novelty and contrast in the message.

E. CHOOSING MEDIA

1. Personal Communication Channels - involve two or more people in direct communication. Word of mouth (WOM) is especially credible to consumers - either positive or negative.

2. Non-personal Communication Channels - include major media such as print, broadcast and display. Atmospheres are designed environments that create or reinforce the buyer's leanings to buy a product. Events are occurrences staged to communicate messages to target audience.

F. EVALUATING & COLLECTING FEEDBACK
Effective feedback measures involves asking the target audience whether they saw the message, when, how many times and what about the message they recall.

A SHORT CHECKLIST FOR MONITORING PROMOTION

DOES YOUR PROMISE OFFER:
- Hope
- Reassurance
- Identification
- Pleasure
- Cognition
- Reward
- Superiority
- Value
- Compatibility

DOES YOUR MESSAGE HAVE:
- Impact
- Involvement
- Recall
- Image
- Credibility

DOES A PURCHASE SUGGEST:
- Ego gratification
- Maternal traits
- Romantic rewards
- Emotional Security
- Social acceptability
- Required recognition
- Self-esteem
- Winning ways

DOES YOUR ADVERTISEMENT:

A. Attract Attention
   Arouse Interest
   Stimulate Desire
   Compel Action

B. Create Awareness
   Ensure Conviction
   Reach an Audience
   Inspire Action

REAL ADVERTISEMENTS THAT APPEARED IN THE U.S. PRESS !!!

1. Illiterate? Write today for free help.

2. Auto Repair Service. Free pick-up and delivery. Try us once, you'll never go anywhere again.

3. Our experienced Mom will care for your child. Fenced yard, meals and smacks included.

4. Dog for sale: eats anything and is fond of children.

5. Man wanted to work in dynamite factory. Must be willing to travel.

6. Stock up and save. Limit: one.

7. Semi-annual After-Christmas sale.

8. 3-year old teacher needed for pre-school. Experience preferred.

9. Mixing bowl set designed to please a cook with round bottom for efficient beating.

10. Dinner special - Turkey $2.35; Chicken or Beef $2.25; Children $2.00.

MARKETING MANAGEMENT

TOPIC: ADVERTISING
LECTURE: 15

ADVERTISING

Advertising is the most visible part of promotion. It refers to any paid form of nonpersonal presentation and promotion of ideas, goods, services, persons or places through the mass media such as newspapers, magazines, television or radio by an identified sponsor.

The Evolution of Advertising.
Mass advertising did not really begin until the mid-1800s. The first advertising agencies did not create ads at all; these firms were media brokers who earned a living by charging a fee in return for negotiating rates with newspapers for placing other people's messages. As magazines began to come on the scene, they helped companies to prepare their ads and create more elaborate messages backing them up with attention-getting artwork and photos. Eventually, they formed agencies and grew closer to the advertisers than to the media.

THE IMPORTANCE OF ADVERTISING TO THE MARKETING FUNCTION
Advertising is likely to play a central role in the promotion mix under the following conditions:
- If the good or service is simple and/or inexpensive and it does not require two-way communication to explain how it works.
- If the good or service is at an early stage in its life cycle and the goal is to build primary demand, intensive advertising that provides necessary information about it is required to convince customers of the need for the product.
- If the good or service is well-established and is competing for acceptance with other mature brands, advertising that focuses on building and reinforcing brand image and differentiating the product from its competition is required to attain or hold high market share.
- If the good or service is a personal product or one that is valued primarily for its symbolic rather than its functional qualities, advertising is often an effective way to create a desirable brand personality.

LIMITATIONS OF ADVERTISING AS A FORM OF PROMOTION.
- *Technology gives power back to the people*. Modern technology has given consumers remote controls for their television sets, VCRs to record and play-back programs or to watch movies and cable television with its proliferation of station choices. Thus television advertising no longer reaches the captive audiences it did in previous decades.
- *Greater emphasis on Point-of-Purchase factors*. Many companies have realised that numerous purchase decisions are only made once the consumer is actually in a store. These factors have contributed to a shift in emphasis away from advertising and toward other elements of the promotion mix e.g. in-store sales promotions and publicity events.
- *The rules are changing in the industry*. Once-loyal clients are turning to computer wizards and even to talent agencies for help in developing communications programs.
- *Advertising is Expensive!*
- *The advertising environment is very cluttered.*
- *Advertising turns off some consumers.*

IMPORTANT TRENDS AFFECTING THE ADVERTISING INDUSTRY.

- **Technology.** Many agencies are banking on new technology to deliver advertising messages (such as the WWW, electronic mail, cable, and interactive media), often with a goal of personalising the message.
- **Global Reach.** Advertisers are trying to establish brand images globally. Fast and clear satellite transmission improves global marketing, and many executives now understand that to compete in the 1990s and beyond they must broaden their focus as consumers in one country increasingly are exposed to and influenced by what happens to people elsewhere.
- **Diversity.** Organisations are working hard to better reflect the cultural diversity of their target markets by including many different types of people in their advertising.
- **Integrated Communications Strategies.** An emphasis on Integrated Marketing Communications (IMC) is reminding many that advertising strategies need to be developed that work in harmony with other aspects of a company's overall marketing strategy.

TYPES OF ADVERTISING

- **Product Advertising** is intended to persuade people to choose a specific product or service.

- **Business-to-Business Advertising** is widely used by manufacturers to communicate with businesses and organisations. This form of communication is relied upon by producers of goods and services, retailers, wholesalers and even governments.

- **Institutional Advertising** promotes the activities, "personality," or point of view of an organisation.
    1. **Corporate Image Advertising** is designed to create a corporate identity, the overall image of the organisation held by members of society.
    2. **Retail Advertising** is usually local rather than national. It typically consists of brand-related product information that focuses on the items carried by a store. The primary goal of retail advertising, especially that placed by local retailers is to build store traffic rather than to increase the consumer's brand awareness.
    3. **Public Service Advertising** (PSAs) sell causes rather than products or companies. One variation of public service advertising is advocacy advertising, or cause advertising. This is an attempt by an organisation to influence public opinion on an issue in which it has some stake in the outcome.

THE ADVERTISING CAMPAIGN.

An advertising campaign is a co-ordinated, comprehensive communications plan that is tied to promotion objectives and results in a series of messages placed in different media over a specified time period. This section will describe the duties of the major players who must work together to make a campaign happen, and discuss how the nature of a campaign depends upon the objectives of the advertiser.

An advertiser or client can be a manufacturer or a service provider, a distributor or retailer, or an institution. Individuals are often advertisers as well. In some cases large firms, wishing for closer control over their advertising, maintain an in-house agency that actually creates the company's advertising.

An advertising agency creates a communication on behalf of a client and delivers it to a target market as efficiently and creatively as possible through:

1. ***Account Management***. The account executive is the "soul" of the operation. He or she is in charge of developing the overall strategy for the client and ensuring that the advertising that is created will meet the client's desired objectives.
2. ***Creative Services***. These are the people who actually dream up and produce the ads. They include the agency's creative director (who is in charge of ensuring that the agency's strategy is expressed in the most interesting and effective way), the copywriter, art director, and producer.
3. ***Research and Marketing Services***. They collect and analyse information that will help account executives develop a sensible strategy. They assist 'creatives' in designing and evaluating ad executions by doing copy testing to gauge consumer reactions to different versions of ads, or by providing copywriters with details on the target group that allow them to have a better picture of who will be exposed to the advertising and what will appeal to them.
4. ***The Account Planner*** is a fairly new position that is gaining in popularity. The planner is not attached to a department, but instead works with researchers and creatives to be sure that ads will appeal to the target market.
5. **Media Planning.** The media planner helps to determine which communications vehicles will be the most effective at accomplishing the campaign's advertising objectives.

MAJOR DECISIONS IN ADVERTISING

A. SETTING OBJECTIVES

The basic reasons for developing the campaign need to be tied to the marketing plan for advertising to work. Ideally, all of the specific advertising executions will be consistent with this plan. One basic strategic issue revolves around what the advertising is supposed to accomplish in terms of reinforcing or changing the way consumers think about or act toward the product, service, or idea.

Advertising objectives are specific communications tasks to be accomplished for a specific target audience during a specified time period. Advertising objectives can be to **inform** (build primary demand), **persuade** (selective demand), or **remind** (brand loyalty). Advertising objectives are often linked to specific communication and sales objectives.

An important goal of advertising is to create awareness by getting peoples attention and motivating them to think about the good or service and how it would fit into their lives. Once a product has been established, advertising focuses on building selective demand, which involves creating desire for one brand over others in its category.

For an advertising message to be effective, it should satisfy four requirements that are commonly lumped together in a formula known as AIDA:
- Attention
- Interest
- Desire
- Action

A creative platform is a document that lays out the strategy decisions for a specific ad. It includes the basic elements of the advertising strategy, such as target audience and objectives.

B. SETTING THE ADVERTISING BUDGET

Advertising budgets are set for each product consistent with the advertising objectives. Four commonly used methods for setting the advertising budget are the following:
- Affordable method
- Percentage-of-sales method
- Competitive-parity method
- Objective-and-task method

To implement objectives, budgets must be set in consideration of the product's position in terms of:
- ***Stage in the product life cycle*** New products typically receive large advertising budgets to build awareness and to gain consumer trial. Established brands usually are supported with lower budgets as a ratio to sales.
- ***Market share and consumer base*** High-market-share brands usually require less advertising expenditures as a percentage of sales to maintain their share. To build share by increasing market size requires larger advertising expenditures. On a cost-per-impression basis, it is less expensive to reach consumers of a widely used brand than to reach consumers of low-share brands.
- ***Competition and clutter*** In a market with a large number of competitors and high advertising spending, a brand must advertise more heavily to be heard above the noise in the market. Even simple clutter from advertisements not directly competitive to the brand creates a need for heavier advertising.
- ***Advertising frequency*** The number of repetitions needed to put across the brand's message to consumers also determines the advertising budget.
- ***Product substitutability*** Brands in a commodity class (e.g. cigarettes, beer, soft drinks) require heavy advertising to establish differential usage. Advertising is also important when a brand can offer unique physical benefits or features, which must be communicated.

ADVERTISING STRATEGY = Creating the Advertising Message + Selecting the Media

---

C. CREATING THE ADVERTISING MESSAGE
- ***Message Generation*** - consists of creative brainstorming to generate several alternative ways of communicating to the target market.
- ***Message Evaluation and Selection*** - ranks and then chooses among message on the how meaningful, distinctive, and believable they are.
- ***Message Execution*** - involves determining how to best communicate with the target market including tone, style, word choice, and format for the ads.

An advertising appeal is the central idea of the message. Most appeals can be described in terms of their overall emphasis on facts versus feelings.

The Steak: Hard Sell. A hard sell is an appeal that reflects a product-centred strategy; it presents information about the item in order to influence the receiver's beliefs about how the product functions or what tangible benefits it can deliver.
- Some of the most effective hard sell appeals simply present a Unique Selling Proposition (USP) - they give consumers one clear reason why one product is better.
- Comparative Advertising is where two or more brands are compared by name.

The Sizzle: Soft Sell. A soft sell appeal is more indirect. It attempts to create an emotional response in the receiver that will translate into desire for the product.
- Fear Appeals highlight the negative consequences of using or not using a product.
- Celebrity Endorsements. The use of celebrity endorsers is a common but expensive strategy. It is particularly effective for mature products that need to differentiate themselves from competitors.
- Many ads appear to be selling sex rather than products.
- Humorous Appeals are most effective when the brand is clearly identified, the jokes are appropriate to the product, and the ad does not make fun of the consumer.

Execution styles
- *Slice of life* One or more people using the product in a normal setting
- *Lifestyle* Emphasises how a product fits in with lifestyle
- *Fantasy* Creates fantasy around product or its use
- *Mood or image* Builds evocative mood or image around the product, such as beauty love or serenity
- *Musical* Uses background music or shows one or more people or cartoon characters singing a song involving the product
- *Personality symbol* Creates a character that personifies the product
- *Technical expertise* Shows the company's expertise and experience in making the product
- *Scientific evidence* Presents survey or scientific evidence that the brand is preferred or outperforms other brands
- *Testimonial evidence* Features a highly credible, likeable, or expert source endorsing the product

D. SELECTING ADVERTISING MEDIA

Media Strategy focuses on the characteristics of different media alternatives that make them attractive or unattractive in terms of their relative ability to efficiently deliver the advertising message to the target market and the choices available to the media planner in terms of how to schedule these messages.

Media Planning is a problem-solving process directed toward placing a message before a target audience in the most effective fashion.

1. Deciding on Reach, Frequency, and Impact.
In selecting media for ads, advertisers must consider the reach (% exposed), frequency (number of times), and impact (qualitative effect) of the various media types, then specify which media vehicles to be used at what time (media timing).
- **Exposure** is the degree to which an advertising message placed in a specific vehicle will be seen or heard by members of a target market. To calculate the exposure a message will have if placed in a certain medium, planners measure exposure by considering two factors: reach and frequency.
- **Reach** is the proportion of the target market that will be exposed to the media vehicle.
- **Frequency** is the number of times a given person in a target group would be expected to be exposed to the message.
- **Gross Rating Points.** The estimated GRPs for the media is simply measured by multiplying reach times frequency. Media planners use a measure called cost per

thousand (CPM), which allows them to compare vehicles that have different exposure rates. CPM is calculated as:

$$CPM = \frac{\text{Cost of message unit} \times 1000}{\text{Number of exposures}}$$

2. **Choosing Among Major Media Types.** Here the marketer must consider the media habits of the target consumer, the nature of the product, and the different types of messages needed to promote the product.

Types of Media.

1. *Broadcast Media.* Broadcast media include television and radio. Radio is gaining popularity as an advertising medium due to its low cost and its ability to target specific consumer segments. A radio campaign can reinforce a brand's other advertising efforts by adding local flavour.

2. *Print Media.* The drop in readership has forced papers to rethink their relationships with marketers. Some are exploring alternative ways to deliver information, and are getting into electronic publishing, database marketing, and other emerging forms of communication.

Magazines have adapted to changing times by focusing their appeals to more specific segments. New technologies such as selective binding allow publishers to personalise their editions, and desktop publishing allows magazines to close their pages just before going to press, eliminating the long lead time that used to be a serious drawback for advertisers who wanted to hit their market with timely information.

3. *Out-of-Home Media* refers to communications vehicles that reach people in public places, such as billboards, blimps, and transit ads placed on buses and subways. Out-door advertising works best when there is a simple, straightforward message and a lot of details are not necessary to tell the story. Place-based media, whether in the form of signs or of closed-circuit video presentations attempt to reach a captive audience.

4. *Direct and Interactive Media.* Direct media appear in both broadcast and print form, including television shopping, computerised services and electronic mail, FAX advertising, and messages on the Internet as well as catalogues, letters, and flyers.

Analysing and Comparing Media Effectiveness. The planner's task is to create a media schedule that specifies the exact media to be used and when (including how often) the messages will be sent. The media planner considers such information as:
- the match between the demographic and psychographic profile of the target audience and the people reached by a media vehicle
- sales patterns to analyse media in terms of area differences and month-by-month differences, as well as distribution of the brand.
- the advertising patterns of competitors
- the amount of attention viewers or readers will pay to material appearing in each alternative.
- the capability of a medium to adequately convey the desired information.
- the quality of the media environment.

3. **Selecting Specific Media Vehicles.** This involves selecting the particular newspaper, magazine, or television show to use within each type of media.

4. Deciding on Media Timing.

When the media schedule is selected, planners are making decisions about the overall pattern the advertising will follow. The following three patterns are typical.

- **Continuous schedule** means maintaining a steady stream of advertising throughout the year.
- **Pulsing schedule** means that some advertising is continuous throughout the year but the advertising is run more heavily during some times than others.
- **Flighting schedule** is an extreme form of pulsing, where advertising appears in short, intense bursts alternating with periods of little to no activity

E. ADVERTISING EVALUATION

- **Measuring the Communication Effect** - is accomplished by copy testing and may include direct ratings, portfolio testing, or laboratory tests of recall and recognition.
- **Measuring the Sales Effect** - attempts to separate the effect of advertising from other elements in the promotion mix.

MARKETING MANAGEMENT

TOPIC: SALES PROMOTION & PUBLIC RELATIONS
LECTURE: 16

SALES PROMOTION

Sales Promotion is the use of an incentive by marketers to induce defined customer groups (channel members, industrial, end-users) to perform specific actions. Over time, role of sales promotions has changed dramatically from that of a minor component of the promotion mix to a major component of promotion mix

Key factors contributing to the increased use of sales promotion include:
- Top management acceptance of sales promotion as an effective element in the marketing mix
- Increased competition and decreased differentiation
- Decreased advertising effectiveness has also put pressure on companies to shift more emphasis to sales promotion.

The specific purposes of Sales Promotion vary according to certain needs, such as breaking down customer loyalty when trying to entice new users. Most analysts believe sales promotion does not lead to long-term customer loyalty. In any case the overall goal of sales promotion is to contribute to consumer franchise building - helping to effect a long-term relationship with customers.

ADVANTAGES AND DISADVANTAGES OF SALES PROMOTIONS

Advantages
- Sales promotion is an extremely effective tool for stimulating behavioural response e.g. "Buy Now"

Disadvantages
- Frequent sales promotions can cause customers to perceive a brand as a "deal" brand or in other words, weaken its brand image
- Frequent sales promotions can cause customers to become more deal oriented in the long run

TRADE DIRECTED SALES PROMOTIONS

Generally Trade Directed Sales Promotions have the purpose of affecting:
- Stocking
- Displaying
- Attention to product by trade members marketing activities

The most frequent objectives of trade sales promotions are to:
- Facilitate new product introductions by ensuring product availability and obtaining favourable display
- Limit competitors' access to shelf space

- Move a product whose sales season is coming to an end
- Obtain more favourable display of existing products
- Counter competitors' promotional efforts
- Increase inventory turnover

KEYS TO SUCCESSFUL TRADE SALES PROMOTIONS
- Provision of a desirable incentive
- Timing - Marketers have to consider:
  - Sales seasonality
  - Other promotional activities such as advertising and consumer promotion
- Ease of use for trade intermediaries
- Having fast and measurable results
- Having a favourable and visible impact on trade performance

TYPES OF TRADE PROMOTIONS
The selection of a specific type of trade directed sales promotion is analogous to selection of a specific creative tactic in advertising. In effect this is the creative strategy that will lead to attainment of the marketer's trade sales promotion objectives. Selection depends on the:
- Objectives
- Budget
- Trade co-operation and responsiveness to particular promotions
- Marketers' ability to choose to participate (or not) in a particular promotion

Specific types of frequently used trade sales promotions include:
- Trade allowances - come in a variety of forms but in general are a price reduction or direct financial reward. Categories are:
  1. Buying allowances
  2. Slotting allowances

- Co-operative advertising - marketer pays part (sometimes all) trade intermediaries' advertising cost for featuring their brand prominently

- Training programs - products that require active sales effort at the point of sale often require marketer to conduct training for trade intermediaries' sales forces and to reward them for successful sales efforts

- Trade shows - a very important activity for many marketers
  1. For some industries, the majority of sales are made at trade shows
  2. Great opportunity for competitive intelligence gathering
  3. Good for developing, maintaining and building customer relations
  4. Good for introducing new products and obtaining market feedback

CONSUMER DIRECTED SALES PROMOTIONS
Rewards/incentives for consumer sales promotions are either
- Immediate
- Delayed

General experience is that immediate rewards are more likely to produce consumer response than delayed rewards.

A Classification of Consumer Sales Promotions

CONSUMER REWARD	MARKETER OBJECTIVES		
	Trial Impact	*Brand Franchise Maintenance and/ or Consumer Loading*	*Image Reinforcement*
Immediate	• Sampling • Instant coupons • Shelf delivered coupons	• Price offs • Bonus packs • In on and near pack coupons	
Delayed	• Media and Mail • Free in-mail premiums. • Scanner delivered coupons.	• In and on-pack coupons • Refunds and rebates	• Self liquidating premiums • Contests and sweepstakes

Targets of Sales Promotions and Push-Pull Strategies

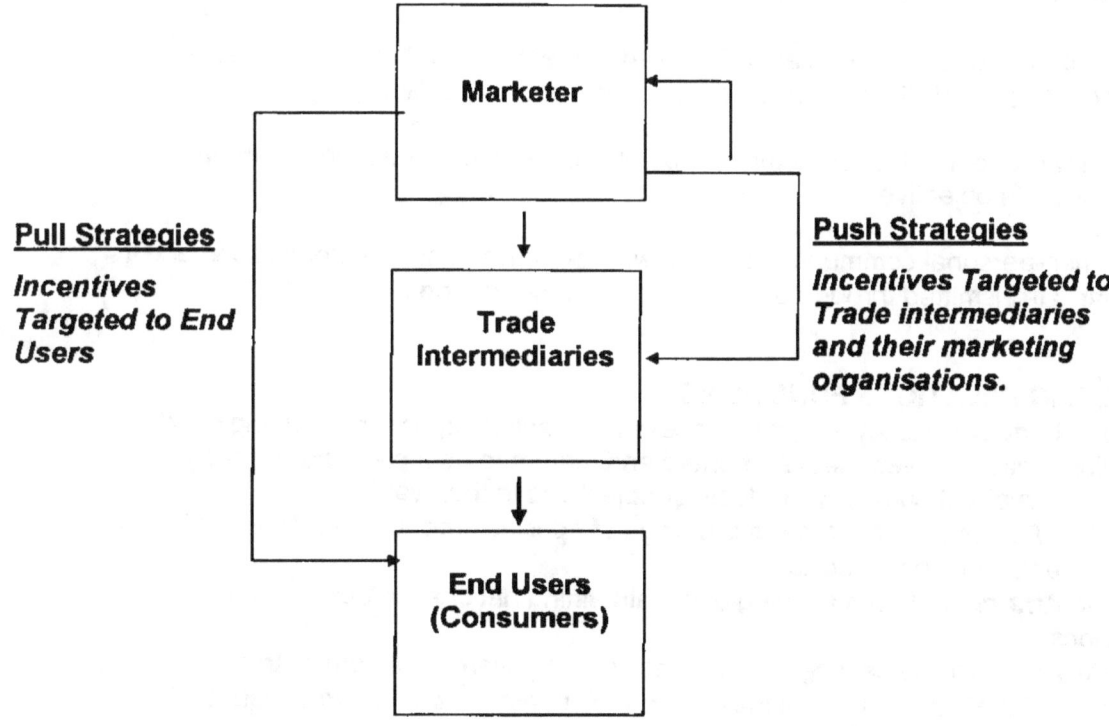

Pull Strategies

Incentives Targeted to End Users

Push Strategies

Incentives Targeted to Trade intermediaries and their marketing organisations.

DEVELOPING THE SALES-PROMOTION PROGRAM

1. **Incentives** - all sales promotions must recognise that a certain minimum level of incentive is needed to have any effect.
2. **Conditions of Participation** - may be both legally mandated in some areas and/or linked to specific goals. Sweepstakes may restrict some participants or be linked to other behaviours such as prior purchases or bulk buys. How to inform participants must also be considered, for example, direct mailing of coupons or placing them on the package.
3. **Length of Time** - considerations must be weighed between too short to have much effect or penetration of the market versus too long so as to lose any sense of immediacy to "act now."
4. **Budget** - Sales promotion budgeting suffers from the same organisational problems faced by marketers in other areas. Percentage of sales approaches are not linked to promotion as generating new sales. Objective based budgeting often fails to consider cost effectiveness.
5. **Pretesting and Implementing** - Sales promotion tools benefit from pretesting their effectiveness prior to implementation. Unfortunately, pretesting is seldom done.
6. **Evaluating the Results** - Consumers may be surveyed or experiments conducted to ascertain the long-term impact of the promotion.

PUBLIC RELATIONS AND PUBLICITY

Public Relations - communication activities used to create and maintain favourable relations and foster goodwill between an organisation and its publics

A **Public** is any group that has an actual or potential interest or impact on a company's ability to achieve its objective

Publicity is non-personal communication in news story form about an organisation and its products that is transmitted through a mass medium at no charge.

MAJOR PUBLIC RELATIONS FUNCTIONS

- *Press Relations* - is an on-going process of establishing and maintaining good relations with the news media reporters and editors to help place newsworthy information about company products or objectives in their vehicles.
- *Product Publicity* - seeks news coverage of specific products usually in conjunction with other promotional efforts.
- *Public Affairs* - involves building and maintaining national or local community relations.
- *Lobbying* - involves dealing with legislators and government administrators.
- *Investor Relations* - involves maintaining relationships with shareholders and others in the financial community.
- *Community Development* - involves working with donors and non-profit organisations to gain of time and money for community projects and programs.

MAJOR PUBLIC RELATIONS DECISIONS

1. **Setting Public Relations Objectives** - is the first order of public relations business. PR must determine what it wants to accomplish and how these objectives support the overall promotion objectives. PR may be used to:
   - Build awareness
   - Build credibility
   - Stimulate the salesforce and dealers
   - Hold down promotion costs
   - Assist in the launch of new products
   - Assist in repositioning a mature product
   - Build up interest in a product category
   - Influence specific target groups
   - Defend products that have encountered public problems
   - Build the corporate image in a way that projects favourably on its products

2. **Choosing Public Relations Messages and Vehicles** - requires that the PR department creates the "story" it wants to tell about the company and finds the appropriate media for transmitting it.

3. **Implementing the Public Relations Plan**

4. **Evaluating Public Relations Results** - of PR efforts is difficult because so much PR is designed to support other promotion efforts. Traditional evaluation includes clipping books counting the number of media exposures.

MAJOR PUBLIC RELATIONS TOOLS

1. **News Release** - a short piece of copy publicising an event or product
2. **Feature Article** - a longer manuscript prepared for a specific publication
3. **Captioned Photograph** - a photo with a brief description of its content
4. **Press Conference** - a meeting used to announce major news events to the press and gain publicity
5. **Speeches** - given by executives can create product and company publicity.
6. **Special Events** - consist of public service activities sponsored and controlled by public relations in-house.
7. **Written Materials** - are used to reach specific target markets and include annual reports and company newsletters.
8. **Audio-visual Materials** - such as films and videotapes, can also be targeted to specific audiences.
9. **Corporate-Identity Materials** - such as logos, stationery, and business cards, can also attract attention.
10. **Public Service Activities** - such as sponsoring a worthy charitable cause in the community.

MARKETING MANAGEMENT

TOPIC: PERSONAL SELLING & SALES MANAGEMENT
LECTURE: 17

PERSONAL SELLING
Personal selling involves the two-way flow of communication between buyer and seller, often in a face-to-face encounter designed to influence a person's or group's purchase decision, but also over highly advanced telecommunication lines.

Personal selling is the interpersonal arm of the promotion mix. The salesforce serves a number of key roles, including: representing the company to customers, representing customers to the company, and assuming leadership in producing customer satisfaction and company profit.

The highly human-intensive nature of personal selling necessitates that people be managed. Sales management involves planning the selling program, as well as implementing and controlling the personal selling effort of the firm.

Virtually every occupation that involves customer contact has an element of personal selling. Many executives in major companies have held sales positions at some time in their careers.

PERSONAL SELLING IN MARKETING
Personal selling serves three major roles in a firm's overall marketing effort:

- Salespeople provide a link between buyer and seller.
- Salespeople represent what a company is or attempts to be.
- Personal selling often plays a dominant role in a firm's marketing program.

The importance of personal selling to the marketing function can be summarised by the following:
- **One Message Per Customer, Please.** Unlike most forms of advertising, personal selling allows for flexible, precisely targeted one-on-one marketing communications.
- **Customers Talk Back.** In direct customer salesperson-interactions, the salesperson can listen to customers and can address objections as well as communicate product benefits.
- **More than Just Communications.** Successful firms need to provide not only communications but also a variety of services for their customers. The sales function allows the firm to provide this extra level of support.
- **Feedback on Marketing Strategy.** The salesperson is an invaluable source of feedback in his or her role as the firm's eyes and ears in the field. They are thus an important source of specific competitive intelligence.

THE EVOLUTION OF PERSONAL SELLING.
During this century, personal selling has done much to redeem itself as a profession as it has moved from a transactional "hard sell" approach to marketing to a relationship marketing approach.

1. **Transactional Marketing**: Putting on the Hard Sell. The hard sell is a high-pressure form of selling. Transactional selling is a form of personal selling that focuses on making an immediate sale-a single transaction-with little or no attempt to develop a relationship with the customer. Hard-sell techniques typically are used to sell products consumers typically buy only once or a few times in their lives. The truly professional salesperson is long-term oriented and works hard to build a relationship with customers.

2. **Relationship Selling** means that the salesperson seeks to develop a mutually satisfying relationship with the customer, one in which the salesperson and the customer work together to satisfy each other's needs. Most selling situations are characterised by long-term relationships because it is more cost-effective by far to keep current customers happy than it is to continually find new customers. The objectives of relationship selling include winning, keeping, and developing customers. The salesperson who practices relationship selling realises both the salesperson and the company will be best served by a style of selling that will stimulate repeat purchases. Relationship selling involves mutual respect and trust that focuses on creating long-term customers, not a one-time sale and commitment to customer needs over time.

FORMS OF PERSONAL SELLING

Personal selling assumes many forms based on the amount of selling done and the amount of creativity required to perform the sales task.

a. An **Order-taker** typically processes routine orders or reorders for products that were already sold by the company. Outside order takers visit customers and replenish inventory. Inside order takers answer simple questions, take orders, and complete transactions with customers.

b. An **Order-getter** sells in a conventional sense and identifies prospective customers, provides customers with information, persuades customers to buy, closes sales, and follows-up on customer experience with a product or service. Another term is **Demand creator** - positions where salespeople have to creatively sell products

c. **Sales support personnel** augment the selling effort of order-getters by performing a variety of services. They do not sell products or services in a conventional sense.

d. **Missionary salespeople** do not strictly solicit orders but rather concentrate on performing promotional activities and introducing new products.

e. **Sales engineers** specialise in identifying, analysing, and solving customer problems and bring technical expertise to the selling situation.

f. **Account service representatives** provide customer service to established accounts

g. **Medical Detailers** - provide doctors with latest information but do not take orders (pharmaceuticals only)

Team selling is the practice of using an entire team of professionals in selling to and servicing major customers. Conference selling involves a salesperson and other company resource people meeting with buyers to discuss problems and opportunities. In seminar selling, a company team conducts an educational program for a customer's technical staff. IBM and Xerox pioneered cross-functional team selling.

THE SELLING PROCESS

KNOWLEDGES				
YOURSELF	PRODUCTS & SERVICES		PROCEDURES & STRATEGY	MARKET COMPETITION
PREPARATION:	OBJECTIVES & TOOLS			
HANDLING OBJECTIONS	PROSPECTING AND QUALIFYING			ANSWERING QUESTIONS
HANDLING OBJECTIONS	PREAPPROACH			ANSWERING QUESTIONS
HANDLING OBJECTIONS	APPROACH			ANSWERING QUESTIONS
HANDLING OBJECTIONS	PRESENTATION & DEMONSTRATION			ANSWERING QUESTIONS
HANDLING OBJECTIONS	CONCLUSION			ANSWERING QUESTIONS
HANDLING OBJECTIONS	CLOSING			ANSWERING QUESTIONS
FOLLOW - UP				
TECHNOLOGY	SALES			ADMINISTRATION

The personal selling process consists of six stages:

a. **PROSPECTING**. The first stage in this process is prospecting, the search for and qualification of potential customers. There are three types of prospects:
- A lead is the name of a person who may be a possible customer.
- A prospect is a customer who wants or needs the product.
- A qualified prospect is an individual who wants the product, can afford to buy it, and is the decision-maker.

Lead development techniques include:
- Ask current customers
- Cultivate sources of referral
- Join organisations to which prospects belong
- Engage in speaking and writing activities that draw attention
- Examine sources (newspapers, directories) in search of names
- Use the telephone and mail to find leads
- Cold canvassing

b. PREAPPROACH. The preapproach stage involves obtaining further information on the prospect and deciding on the best method of approach. Activities in this stage include finding information on who the prospect is, how the prospect prefers to be approached, and what the prospect is looking for in a product or service.

c. APPROACH. The approach stage involves the initial meeting between the salesperson and prospect where the objectives are to gain the prospect's attention, stimulate interest, and build the foundation for the sales presentation itself.

d. PRESENTATION. The objective of the presentation stage is to convert a qualified prospect into a customer by creating a desire for the product or service. Three major presentation formats exist:

    1. **Stimulus Response Format.** The stimulus-response presentation format assumes that given the appropriate stimulus by a salesperson, the prospect will buy. With this format the salesperson tries one appeal after another, hoping to "hit the right button."

    2. **Formula Selling format.** The formula selling presentation format is based on the view that a presentation consists of information that must be provided in an accurate, thorough, and step-by-step manner to persuade the prospect to buy. A popular version of this f format is the canned sales presentation, where a memorised, standardised message is conveyed to every prospect.

    3. **Need-satisfaction format.** The need satisfaction presentation format emphasises probing and listening by the salesperson to identify needs and interests of prospective buyers. Once identified, the salesperson tailors the presentation to the prospect and highlights product benefits that satisfy the prospect. Adaptive selling and consultative selling approaches are commonly applied.

Handling Objections. Objections are excuses for not making a purchase commitment or a decision. Objections should be handled ethically without lying to or misleading the prospect. Objections can be thought of as a customer's way of testing a salesperson's knowledge about and confidence in the product.

Salespeople need to see objections as an opportunity to provide more information and to turn these issues into reasons for buying. The first two steps of handling objections are crucial.

- First, let the customer know you respect his or her concerns and questions raised by the objection.
- Second, ask about the objection to make sure you and the customer really understand what is at the heart of the objection.

The six most common techniques for handling objections are:
    a. Ignore the objection
    b. Acknowledge and convert the objection
    c. Postpone
    d. Agree and neutralise
    e. Accept the objection
    f. Denial

e. Closing the Sale.
The closing stage involves obtaining a purchase commitment from the prospect. Often it is unclear when the prospect is ready to buy. There are several ways to accomplish this crucial step:

- In a **trial close**, the salesperson acts as if the purchase is inevitable and now the task is just to wrap up the details. It usually takes the form of asking for a decision on some aspect of the purchase
- An **options close** asks the customer to select between alternatives.
- A last **objection close** asks the customer if he or she is ready to purchase, providing this final concern can be addressed.
- An **assumptive close** goes a step further; the salesperson acts as if the purchase has already been made. It entails asking the prospect to make choices concerning the product under the assumption that a sale has been finalised
- A **summary of benefits close** occurs when the salesperson presents a summary of the major benefits of interest to the customer.
- An **urgency close** or **standing-room-only close** means that the salesperson indicates that if the customer does not buy now, he may not have the opportunity in the future.
- A **negotiation close** means that the salesperson seeks to find a mutually agreeable compromise in order to get the sale.
- A **silent close** occurs when the salesperson simply remains silent, waiting for the customer to indicate he wishes to order.

f. **FOLLOW-UP.** The follow-up stage includes making certain that the customer's purchase has been properly delivered and installed and that any difficulties experienced with the use of the item are addressed. The buyer must be assured of the salesman's interest and any cognitive dissonance reduced.

SALES MANAGEMENT

Selling must be managed if it is going to contribute to a firm's overall objectives. Sales management consists of three main interrelated functions:
- Sales plan formulation.
- Sales plan implementation.
- Salesforce evaluation and control.

a. SALES PLAN FORMULATION.

The sales plan is a statement describing what is to be achieved and where and how the selling effort of salespeople is to be deployed. Formulating the sales plan involves three tasks:

1. **Establishing sales force objectives** is the task of specifying what is to be achieved. Selling objectives can be output-related, input-related, or behavioural related. Once established, these objectives serve as performance standards for sales force evaluation - the third function of sales management.

Basically, the issue is how salespeople should allocate their time and efforts among
- Identifying and developing new accounts
- Servicing existing accounts
- Conducting marketing intelligence
- Performing administrative activities
- Participation in other promotional activities
- Professional development

2. **Organising the Salesforce.**
The task of organising the sales force revolves around three questions.

   a. Should the company use its own sales force or should it use independent agents? Here, both economic and behavioural considerations must be weighed before making this decision. Control, flexibility, effort, and availability are important criteria to be considered.

   b. If the decision is made to employ company sales people, then how should they be organised? Typically, an organisational structure is based on geography, customer, product or any combination of these.
   A recent innovation in organisational structure is major account management. This structure is similar to a customer organisational structure and employs a team selling approach. Activities involved are identification, classification and establishing call frequencies for each account category
   - **Account identification** - basically a demand analysis issue to identify accounts and estimate the market size and profitability of each account category developed.
   - **Account classification** - generally accounts are grouped into categories that differ with respect to the market size of each category. Typical grouping is into A, B, C, D, etc. depending upon company and market diversity with A accounts having largest sales market size
   - **Determining call frequencies** on each account category. The issue is deciding how often salespeople should call on customers in each account category.

   c. How many salespeople should be employed? The answer to this question lies in terms of the number of accounts served, the frequency of calls on accounts, the length of an average call, and the amount of time a salesperson can devote to selling. The work load method formula can be used to arrive at a sales force figure:

$$NS = \frac{NC \times CF \times CL}{AST}$$

where: NS = number of salespeople, CF = calls frequency necessary to service a customer each year, NC = number of customers, CL = length of an average call, AST = average amount of selling time available per year

3. **Developing account management policies.**
The task of developing account management policies specifies who salespeople should contact, what kinds of selling and customer service activities should be engaged in, and how these activities should be carried out.

b. SALES PLAN IMPLEMENTATION
Sales plan implementation involves three major tasks:

1. **Sales force recruitment and selection** entails finding people who match the type of sales position required by the firm. This task often begins with creating a job analysis, a written description of relationships and job requirements that detail what a salesperson is expected to do.

2. **Sales force training** typically focuses on two issues: selling skills and product knowledge. Both are important for successful selling. On-the-job training is the most popular type of training.

3. **Sales force motivation and compensation** Research suggests that
    - a clear job description
    - effective sales management practices
    - a sense of achievement, and
    - proper incentives and rewards will produce a motivated salesperson.

Pay is generally the most important motivating factor, and salespeople are generally paid using one of three plans:

a. Straight salary compensation plan: salesperson is paid a fixed fee per week, month, or year.

b. Straight commission compensation plan: salesperson's earnings are tied directly to the sales or profits generated.

c. Combination compensation plan: salesperson's income comes from a specified salary plus a commission on sales or profit generated.

A summary of the Roles of different types of Compensation.

Element	Roles and Uses
Fixed Salary	Encourages non-selling activities such as administrative work, attending trade shows, missionary sales work.
Commission	Motivates sales people to greater effort, can generate new account development if existing accounts are tapped out. One approach to using commissions to spur new accounts development is to offer higher commissions on first year sales to new accounts won and retained.
Bonuses	Can be used in many ways to stimulate sales efforts.

c. SALESFORCE EVALUATION AND CONTROL

Sales force evaluation involves the assessment of whether sales objectives were met and account management policies were followed. Both quantitative and behavioural measures are used.

- Quantitative assessments are based on input- and output-related objectives set forth in the sales plan. The most frequently used input-related objective is the number of calls made. Sales volume is the major output-related objective.
- Behavioural evaluation typically includes subjective and often informal assessments of a salesperson's attitude, product knowledge, selling and communication skills, appearance, and demeanour. However, these subjective factors often do determine whether quantitative input- related and output-related objectives are met.

Sources of Information for evaluating salespeople

1. *Sales Reports* are the most important source of information managers have on their salesforce.

2. *Work Plans* are submitted and describe the calls and routing for the coming week or month.

3. **Annual Territory Marketing Plans** are outlines for building new accounts and increasing sales.
4. **Call Reports** log sales calls.
5. **Expense Reports** provide information on activity and expenses to be reimbursed.

Formal Evaluation of Performance

1. **Comparing Salespeople's Performance.** Comparisons are helpful although many other factors influence performance such as differing conditions in each territory.
2. **Comparing Current Sales With Past Sales.** Past sales help identify trends. Interpretation is needed to evaluate trends with company expectations.
3. **Qualitative Evaluation of Salespeople.** These subjective evaluations look at a salesperson's knowledge of the company, products, customers, competitors, territory, and tasks.

SALESFORCE AUTOMATION

Salesforce automation is the use of technology designed to make the sales function more effective and efficient. Computer and communication technologies have and will continue to play a central role in salesforce automation.

- **Salesforce computerisation.** Computer technology has become an integral part of field selling through innovations such as laptop, notebook, palmtop, pad, and tablet computers.
- **Salesforce communication.** Technology has changed the way salespeople communicate with customers, other salespeople and sales support personnel, and management. Facsimile, electronic mail, voice mail, and cellular phones have made possible the mobile sales office.

A well-designed and well-managed sales force is a tremendous asset. The key is for top management to actively guide design of the sales force and monitor sales force management so that sales objectives are attained. In general, the organisation's goal is to have a sales force that is designed and managed so as to attain sales objectives while minimising sales costs and sales force turnover.

MARKETING MANAGEMENT

TOPIC: CUSTOMER SATISFACTION & CARE
LECTURE: 18

BUILDING CUSTOMER SATISFACTION

The marketing concept is reinterpreted, stressing the need to offer real customer value and customer satisfaction in order to compete effectively

CUSTOMER SATISFACTION
Customer satisfaction is
- need reduction
- the level of a person's felt state resulting from comparing a product's perceived performance (or outcome) in relation to that person's expectations

Customer satisfaction with a purchase depends upon the product's performance relative to a buyer's expectations.

CUSTOMER VALUE
Customer Value is the
- amount of benefit(s) received relative to the cost of that (those) benefit(s)
- bundle of benefits customers expect from a given product or service relative to the amount paid for that bundle of benefits

Customer Delivered Value is defined as the difference between total customer value and total customer cost.
- Total Customer Value - is derived from the product, services, personnel, and image of the offer made by a company.
- Total Customer Cost - includes the buyer's monetary payment, anticipated time, energy, and psychic costs spent in acquisition.

THE VALUE CHAIN
Every firm is a collection of activities that are performed to design, produce, market, deliver, and support its product(s). Porter identifies competitive advantage as derived from a firm's generic value chain consisting of five primary activities and four support activities that create value and cost in a specific business

The five primary activities that he identifies are:
1. *Inbound logistics* which are the activities that are concerned with the reception, storing and internal distribution of the raw materials or components for assembly.
2. *Operations* which turn these into the final product.
3. *Outbound logistics* which distribute the product or service to customers. In the case of a manufacturing operation, this would include warehousing, materials handling and transportation. For a service this would involve the way in which customers are brought to the location in which the service is to be delivered.
4. *Marketing and sales* which make sure the customers are aware of the product or service and are able to buy it.
5. *Service* activities which include installation, repair and training.

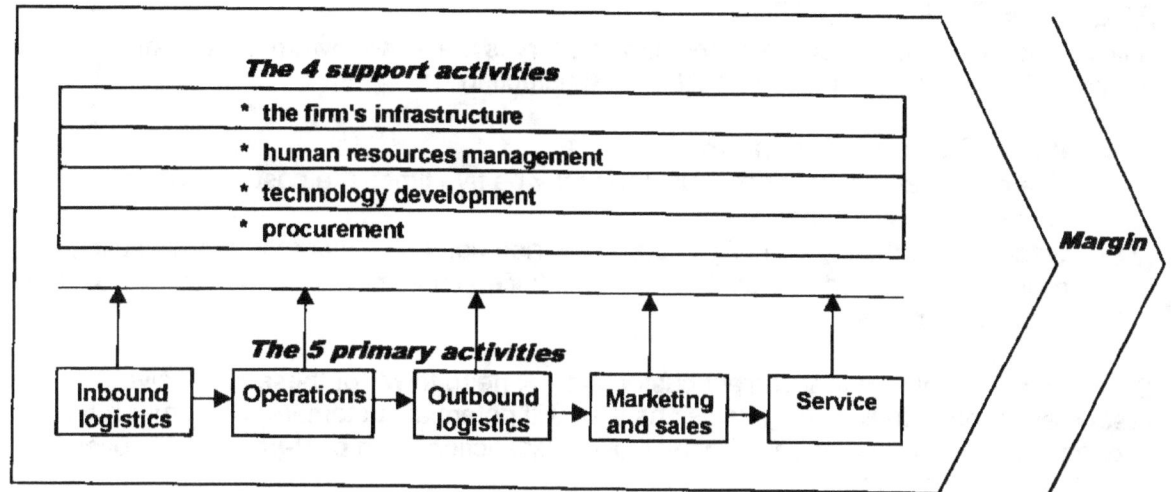

The Value Chain (M. Porter)

Each of these primary activities is, in turn, linked to the support activities which are grouped under four headings.
- **The procurement** of the various resource inputs.
- **Technology development**, including research and development, process improvements and raw material improvements.
- **Human resource management** including the recruitment, training, development and rewarding of staff.
- **The firm's infrastructure** and the approach to organisation including the systems, structures, managerial cultures and ways of doing business.

Porter suggests that competitive advantage is determined to a very large extent by how each of these elements is managed and the nature of the interactions between them. For example, In the case of inbound logistics, many organisations have developed just-in-time systems in order to avoid or minimise their stockholding costs. In this way, the value of the activity is increased and the firm's competitive advantage improved.

Co-ordination of activities is achieved by emphasising core business processes over functional departmentalisation. Core Business Processes include product development, inventory management, order-to-payment, and customer service.

THE VALUE DELIVERY SYSTEM
Firms work from their core businesses to extend value to both customers and suppliers to create competitive advantage. A value-delivery system results when the value chains of suppliers, manufacturers, and distributors are linked

In order to provide customer satisfaction the firm must
- design and manage a superior value-delivery system to reach target customer segments.
- implement Total Quality Management (TQM)

RELATIONSHIP MARKETING

A key trend in marketing for the twenty-first century is the trend toward the use of relationship marketing to improve customer satisfaction.

The Need for Customer Retention

- The cost of attracting a new customer may be five times the cost of keeping a current customer happy
- Offensive marketing typically costs more than defensive marketing because it requires must effort and cost to induce satisfied customers to switch away from their current suppliers

Common sense tells us that current customers will need fewer of these expensive resources to make their buying decisions than will potential customers. Customer retention is enhanced by focusing on relationships over transactions and post-sale activity over presale and sale activity.

Customer defections can have a significant impact on profits because:
1. For each new customer, there are up front costs, such as advertising, credit checking, selling time.
2. The longer a customer stays with a company, the less the effect of these up front costs have on profitability, when spread over the life of the relationship with the customer
3. If customers are served correctly, they also generate more profit each year, for two reasons:
    - As customers become increasingly familiar with a service, they use it more regularly.
    - As purchases rise, the cost of serving the customer reduces (i.e. via experience effects)
4. Loyal customers tend to provide free advertising and referrals, if they are happy with the service they provide. If customers defect, they take all that profit potential with them.

Relationship Marketing involves creating, maintaining, and enhancing strong relationships with customers and other stakeholders.

Relationship Marketing is based on the premise that important accounts need focused and continuous attention and the building of structural, financial and social ties. Salespeople working with key customers must do more than call when they think a customer might be ready to place an order. They also should monitor each key account, know its problems, and be ready to serve in a number of ways.

STEPS IN RELATIONSHIP BUILDING

1. Identify the key customers meriting relationship marketing
2. Assign a skilled relationship manager to each key customer
3. Develop a clear job description of relationship managers
4. Appoint an overall manager to supervise the relationship managers
5. Each relationship manager must develop long-range and annual customer-relationship plans
6. Appoint an overall manager to supervise the relationship managers.

Profitable Customer: a person, household, or company that yields a revenue stream over timer, exceeding by an acceptable amount the company cost stream (over the life of that customer) of attracting, selling, and servicing that customer

When the revenues of each customer are factored in, it is possible to determine the customer's lifetime value -- the amount of profit generated each year for the company over the lifetime of that customer's business with the company.

Strong customer loyalty can be created by developing Relationship Marketing to high levels. Companies have varying levels of relationships with their customers:
- **Basic Selling** - The salesperson sells the product but does not contact the customer again
- **Reactive Selling** - The salesperson sells the product and encourages the customer to call if he or she has any questions or complaints
- **Accountable Selling** - The salesperson phones the customer a short time after the sale to check whether the product is meeting the customer's expectations. The salesperson also solicits from the customer any product improvement suggestions and any specific disappointments. This information helps the company continuously improve its offering
- **Proactive Selling** - The company salesperson phones the company from time to time with suggestions about improved product use or helpful new products
- **Partnership Building** - The company works continuously with the customer to discover ways to effect customer savings or help the customer perform better

CUSTOMER CARE

Customer care has become recognised as a critical factor in the success of a business, whether it is concerned with providing services or selling products.

Customer care or, as it is sometimes called, the 'service dimension', has become the focus of a new approach for organisations. The delivery of extra 'added value' through the service dimension is a critical competitive factor in market places that are becoming more crowded and more competitive by the day.

Sometimes these service dimensions of the product are referred to as the 'augmented product' and the 'potential product'. Obviously the basic or 'core product' itself needs to function effectively and be well designed, etc. But by concentrating on the augmented and potential product companies pursuing the customer-care strategy can create totally new products heavily oriented towards customer care.

- The 'augmented product' refers to the extra elements aiming to provide additional customer satisfaction - helpful and well trained sales people, range of products provided, guarantees of delivery and responsiveness to customer needs, having 'just the right' flavour, colour, price, etc.

- The 'potential product' refers to the extra dimensions of customer care companies develop, e.g. no quibble refund, return-anything policies; extra high quality decor or extra value provided in service encounters by, for example, music, flowers or entertainment in the service environment; and sensitivity to customer needs, and empowerment of staff to deal with them without referring to higher levels of management. These are all aspects of 'potential product'.

THE NATURE OF CUSTOMER CARE

Customer care is a widely used term, yet definitions of precisely what it covers vary quite a lot. Sometimes the term is used interchangeably with 'customer service'. Customer service developed from a focus on 'order-cycle' related activities into a much more general and all-embracing approach, which covers activities at the pre-, during- and post-transaction stages.

Customer care is the preferred term when we are forced to consider activities beyond direct contact with the customer. It has been described as 'the ultimate marketing tool', and a critical factor in the process of differentiating products or services, to develop a competitive edge. It calls for what some have called the management and identification of 'moments of truth' - contacts between companies and customers where a firm's reputation is at stake. Interaction is still a critical dimension, and the focus has moved away from specific activities to look in general holistic ways at customer satisfaction.
Customer care is aiming to close the gap between customers' expectations and their experience.

Customer care necessitates a culture change within a business. It is not an adjunct to company strategy but a core value that must form the basis for all policy - making and strategic thinking. The difference between 'customer care' and the more traditional notion of 'customer service' seems to lie in the degree of centrality this is given within the process of formulating corporate policies, objectives and strategies

Modern strategic marketing begins and ends with the consumer, yet customer care may well be overlooked in the pursuit of broader, more abstract objectives. The marketing concept expresses a particular business philosophy and provides an analysis of the nature of consumption, consumers, and markets today, placing a central importance on the formulation of strategies that take account of their characteristics. It is, in that sense, focused on consumers as they exist within their environments and as target groups.

The customer-care concept is a principle to guide the formulation of processes and practices within the organisation that can unify and integrate the activities of all organisational members. In a sense, the customer-care concept expresses as a corporate mission the strategic objectives of a marketing orientation.

QUALITY

Marketing by is being redefined in terms of quality and building value-laden, profitable relationships with customers. A seller delivers quality whenever that seller's product or service meets or exceeds the expectations of most of its customers most of the time.

Quality is the totality of features and characteristics of a product or service that bear on its ability to satisfy stated or implied needs

Performance Quality refers to the level at which a product performs its functions.

Conformance Quality refers to freedom from defects and the consistency with which a product delivers a specified level of performance.

TOTAL QUALITY MANAGEMENT (TQM)

Briefly, 'quality' in management can be defined as combining the satisfaction of customer needs with the achievement of company objectives.

The following areas are connected in systems aiming to achieve success and profitability by placing the customer at the centre of all enterprise activities through providing the right amount of the following:
- Quality
- Availability (at launch and afterwards)
- Service
- Support
- Reliability
- Cost/value for money

Such programmes must be 'total', reaching forward to distributors down the chain, and back to suppliers in the case of manufactured goods, to ensure the quality of raw materials and the condition of the product that reaches the ultimate consumer. Hence, Total Quality Management.

PURSUING A TOTAL QUALITY MARKETING STRATEGY

1. **Quality is in the eyes of the customer.** A quality program must begin with the customer's needs and end with customer perceptions.
2. **Quality must reflect every company activity.** Each functional area and each company activity must understand and embody the total quality concept. A system cannot consistently deliver quality if one or more of its components is not operating effectively.
3. **Quality requires total employee commitment.** All company employees must be personally committed to the total quality program. Commitment requires both professional and personal pride in the outcome.
4. **Quality requires high-quality partners.** Value chain members of the customer delivery system must also embody total quality commitment.
5. **A quality program cannot save a poor product.** Companies must recognise that poor product cannot be "quality imaged" successfully. If the product cannot be changed, it should be dropped.
6. **Quality can always be improved.** Nothing is ever perfect.
7. **Quality improvement may require quantum leaps.** Competitive conditions may demand vast and immediate improvements over small and incremental ones.
8. **Quality does not cost more.** Cost savings come from lower rejection rates, better customer satisfaction, and often new technologies that reduce manufacturing costs.
9. **Quality is necessary but may not be sufficient.** More demanding buyers have ever-higher expectations for performance. Companies cannot assume that quality alone will be competitive.

QUALITY AND CUSTOMER CARE

As with quality programmes in general, TQM gives central place to the customer. Satisfying them is the first principle of TQM since they are the guarantee of the organisation's continued existence. Gaining custom means winning a competition for the patronage of each individual or corporate buyer, and satisfying the particular needs of that individual is the competitive edge that wins survival and prosperity.

All products and service attributes that contribute value to the customer and lead to customer satisfaction and preference must be the foundation for a company's quality system. Value, satisfaction and preference may be influenced by many factors throughout the customers' purchase, ownership and service experiences.

Handling complaints, for example, is traditionally seen as 'fire-fighting' or deflecting customers who might cause trouble - squashing them, deflating them, placating them, or keeping them quiet. This orientation demands that these avenues should be opened up, extended and treated as a very serious means of gathering important business information, which requires action. Rather than 'applying plasters', complaints should be the occasion for 'fault detection', so that recurrence can be avoided by getting it right first time. There should also, equally importantly, be means for customer credit to be transmitted to the staff. Staff should not only be aware of customers as potential sources of trouble for them, but also as the barometer for their achievements.

Three principles guide customer-supplier relationships under TQM:
- Recognition of the strategic importance of customers and suppliers.
- Development of win-win relations between customers and suppliers.
- Establishing relations based on trust.

These principles are translated into practices by:
- Constantly collecting information on customer expectations.
- Disseminating this information widely within the organisation.
- Using this information to design, produce and deliver the organisation's products and services.

DELIVERING ADEQUATE LEVELS OF CUSTOMER CARE

1. Produce an adequate definition of the corporate mission
Without clear definition of corporate goals, the business will always be wasting resources and effort through lack of a clear focus and consistent goals. A mission statement has as one of its fundamental aims, however, the communication of purpose to each member of the organisation - it must be easily understood by every participant - and it must also inform individuals how their roles within the organisation contribute towards the achievement of this mission. It therefore has a key role in motivation, and if it is not clearly and effectively formulated, the chance of establishing a customer-care ethos or 'culture' within the organisation is seriously diminished.

2. Use up-to-date and reliable information
Assumptions about what it is that customers want, and notions that it is 'obvious' which product attributes are most important to the customers, are all too common, and frequent causes of dissatisfaction. Information about customers should come from customers, or from those who are closest to them in delivering a product or service.

Information about competitive activity, about changes in market conditions and even about the performance and perception of the company itself, should come from sources that are in touch with the recent reality of the situation, and not dependent on remote or potentially partial individuals or organisations. Unless the company places a very high priority on the gathering, analysis, and dissemination of information to inform decision-making, and also engenders a culture in which information flows freely and is available in a form that can be readily used by decision-makers at all levels, it is difficult to see the organisation developing the degree of openness and responsiveness that is such an integral part of the customer-care concept.

3. Use Information to inform decisions and planning

Too much information is gathered ritualistically or simply because it seems like a good or useful thing to do. When information about customer needs is gathered, it must be used to make effective decisions, and placed at the heart of the planning process. If the information being gathered is not used in this way, the organisation needs to ask why it is being gathered at all.

An important part of this informational system are the mechanisms by means of which this information can be gathered, stored, analysed, disseminated and rendered into forms that decision-markers can relate to their particular concerns. Since customer care is essentially founded, on 'listening' above all else, but also on 'measuring' and 'reacting', or learning from what our information can tell us about what customers think and want, decisions must be information-based in the case of even the most experienced and able managers.

4. Act quickly

Information decays quickly. Failing to act on the basis of information that is available now, and acting after the information has ceased to be relevant, is equally damaging and inappropriate. Customer needs and standards change very quickly in some markets, and when action is needed, it should be taken as quickly as possible.

5. Use written plans that are understandable and achievable, and provide motivation for staff

Written plans should aim to meet communication objectives. If they are written for staff to implement, they should aim to provide a basis on which practical actions can be taken, effects can be identified and measured, and staff achievements can be formulated.

Plans are counterproductive if those who are required to live by them feel that they cannot realistically be met, or that meeting them engenders no commitment and offers no reward or sense of achievement if their challenges have been met.

6. Produce regular progress reports on the implementation of the marketing plan

These must be reliable and detailed, and not simply reports on results. Constant attention to progress, adjustment as necessary to changes in conditions and new customer needs, and changes in perception, all require that the marketing plan being followed should form the background to what is done.

7. Make measurement central to the process of implementation

Scores and systems of measurement provide invaluable benchmarks of progress, and provide targets that can be seen to be met, or not.

8. Disseminate a marketing philosophy, but also assign clear responsibility for the marketing function

If everyone's job has marketing aspects, trouble can occur if no one is actually responsible for making it happen. There must be clearly defined responsibilities here, as well as a core commitment to building it into the way in which the organisation functions at all levels.

SUCCESSFUL CUSTOMER-CARE PROGRAMMES

If programmes are to work, the following conditions must be met:

1. ***Staff must be:***
   - Clear about the programme and their role in it.
   - Committed to the programme.
   - Well trained in programme needs.
   - Sufficiently resourced to carry out their roles.
   - Sufficiently skilled to carry out their roles.

2. ***The programme must:***
   - Provide clear benefits for the staff.
   - Be reinforced by top management action, with effective implementation, clear priorities, and sanctions and rewards.

3. ***Management must be:***
   - Informed about progress and effectiveness of staff performance.
   - Provided with regular and appropriate information.
   - The process must support marketing objectives and facilitate the work of staff towards its achievement.

MARKETING MANAGEMENT

> TOPIC: MANAGING MARKETING
> LECTURE: *19*

THE ROLE OF THE MARKETING MANAGER

Marketing managers guide marketing programs and people in the many different activities associated with offering products to markets. Marketers are information conduits, communicating information about products to personal use and business/organisation consumers, and bringing information back to the business about consumers, the competition, and other important factors in the environment.

Marketing Managers guide strategic marketing decision making including identifying, selecting (targeting) and taking advantage of (positioning) market opportunities. They evaluate an organisation's resources and then set appropriate sales, profit, and market objectives.

They may rely on several traditional models of marketing management to provide a framework for decision making such as the BCG Matrix, the GE Matrix and the Ansoff product/market opportunity Matrix.

Product portfolio models may be used to differentiate the relative market share or profit contribution of different products to the business. While product portfolio models may have descriptive value, their prescriptive value is dubious.

Growth decisions in products and markets can be categorised within a product/market opportunity matrix. The four cells of the matrix include a market penetration strategy which calls for increasing sales of existing products among current target markets without changing the products or markets. A market development strategy calls for entering new markets with the same products. A product development strategy calls for changing products, or adding new ones, to existing markets. Diversifying means offering new products to new markets.

Marketing managers are often called mini-general managers because they perform many of the same tasks as a general manager, but only for marketing activities.

THE ROLE OF MARKETING MANAGEMENT

Marketing Management is the analysis, planning, implementation, and control of programs designed to create, build, and maintain mutually beneficial exchanges and relationships with target markets for the purpose of achieving organisational objectives.

Marketing management focuses on managing the operations aspects of all marketing activities. It provides a mechanism for guiding marketing strategy development and implementation and managing processes and people from initial market analysis through post purchase customer satisfaction

Marketing management means making decisions about people, money, technology, and materials through the interlinked processes of planning, implementation, and control. The marketing program is all the various operating marketing plans and activities that represent the total marketing effort at any particular time.

THE PRIMARY TASKS OF MARKETING MANAGEMENT

1. **Evaluating corporate resources**
    - Financial resources:
    - Capital resources:
    - Human resources:
    - Research and development resources:
    - Sources of supply resources:
    - Market resources:

2. **Setting objectives**
    - Sales objectives: total or percentage change in dollars or units produced and sold.
    - Profit objectives: total or percentage change in profits, profit per unit, gross profit, net profit, profits as a percentage of sales, or as a percentage of ROI.
    - Market objectives: any area of the marketing mix, most common = market share.

3. **Organising the marketing effort**
    - Functional structure: Most appropriate for small product mix of similar products.
    - Brand/product manager structure: common among packaged goods firms with extensive product lines. Current trends suggest this structure is too hierarchical.

4. **Establishing marketing strategy**
    - Identifying opportunities: Assess external environment; use MkIS
    - Selecting target markets: Use opportunities identified and market segmentation.
    - Determining product positioning: Internal (cannibalisation) and External (competitive). (Consideration of competitive resource capabilities, target market's values.

5. **Formulating the marketing mix**
    - Differential advantage: at least one unique ability to create customer satisfaction.
    - Consistency among mix factors: i.e., pricing strategy matches image.
    - Feasibility: Implementation matches firm's financial resources.
    - Matching target expectations: mix matches buyer's evaluation and choice criteria.

6. **Forecasting sales**
    - Jury of executive opinion:
    - Top-down forecast:
    - Estimate of total industry sales under various levels of total industry marketing effort.
    - Estimates firm sales as a share of total.
    - Sales force composite estimate (build-up sales forecasting): aggregate individual sales territory forecasts. (benefit of local knowledge,)
    - Trend projections: Projection from quarterly or annual historical data. (purely quantitative and assume conditions constant).
    - Leading indicators (housing starts, unemployment, consumer debt): Useful when a firm's sales are heavily dependent on the general health of the economy.

7. **Controlling and evaluating the marketing function**
   - Establishing performance standards: overall sales and for specific product lines, regions.
   - Controlling performance: Requires rapid access to reliable information. Control can be built in. (pull strategy).
   - Evaluating performance:
   - Micro: All aspects of marketing mix and customer satisfaction (validity)
   - Macro: Total sales, market share, total profits
   - Marketing audit: Extensive evaluation using micro and macro factors

8. **Implementing corrective action**
   - Identify areas not meeting objectives
   - Replace personnel if necessary
   - Alter organisational structure if necessary
   - Adjust objectives if necessary

THE ROLE OF THE MARKETING PLAN

The marketing plan is the blueprint for what marketing is to accomplish over a period of time, usually one year and sometimes two. The marketing plan must be compatible with and complement plans for other operational areas. Marketing plans specify product-market matches, marketing mix tactics, evaluation and control mechanisms, and resource allocations.

A marketing plan for a small business usually is less formal and complex than a marketing plan for a large company. A large company may have hundreds of different marketing plans operating at one time; a small business may have only one marketing plan. There are many advantages to marketing planning. One is that it forces marketers to systematically address issues that affect business success and possibly, survival.

The planning process calls for evaluating the business's customer base. This often reveals that relatively few customers are responsible for most of the sales. This is the 80-20 Rule, where 80 percent of sales are generated by as few as 20 percent of the customers.

IMPLEMENTATION ACTIVITIES

Marketing plans are meaningless unless and until they are implemented. Implementation is the activation of a marketing plan, when people, money, technology, and materials are brought together to execute marketing mix tactics and achieve marketing objectives.

Implementation requires organising people to perform marketing activities. Good implementation cannot save a flawed marketing plan. Three key activities involved in implementation are organising, staffing, and supervising employees.

There is no single marketing organisation structure that fits all businesses equally well. Recent trends toward flattening corporations, reducing the number of layers of bureaucracy, gives greater power to individuals to take responsibility for their jobs and make decisions. In multibusiness corporations, marketing management begins at the top with a corporate level vice president for marketing. Some marketing managers are responsible for marketing in all of the corporation's businesses.

At lower levels, category managers oversee the marketing of entire categories of products with their many different brands. Brand managers are responsible for managing the marketing of one or several related brands. Other forms include marketing managers for geographical territories, consumer targets, or different operations such as personal selling or new product development.

Implementation often is difficult because it involves change and people have a tendency to resist change. Other implementation problems frequently are the result of communication problems and internal disputes over resources.

PROBLEMS IN IMPLEMENTING MARKETING ACTIVITIES
1. Managers fail to realise that marketing implementation is just as important as marketing strategy.
2. Marketing strategy and implementation are related.
3. Marketing strategy and implementation are constantly evolving.
4. The responsibility for marketing strategy and implementation is separated.

COMPONENTS OF MARKETING IMPLEMENTATION
The marketing implementation process has several components - organisational resources, marketing strategy, marketing structure, systems, leadership, and people - which must mesh if implementation is to succeed.

- Systems refer to work processes, procedures, and the way that information is structured.
- The people component refers to the importance of employees in the implementation process.
- Leadership is the art of managing people and involves issues such as employee motivation, communication, and reward policies.
- Shared goals draw the entire organisation together into a single, functioning unit.

APPROACHES TO MARKETING IMPLEMENTATION

INTERNAL MARKETING
External customers are the individuals who patronise a business. Internal customers are the employees who work for a company. The needs of both sets of customers must be satisfied through marketing activities if implementation is to be successful.

Internal marketing is a management philosophy that co-ordinates internal exchanges between the organisation and its employees to better achieve successful external exchanges between the organisation and its customers. It refers to the managerial actions necessary to make all members of the marketing organisation understand and accept their roles in implementing the marketing strategy.

The success of planning is not the production of plans, but their successful implementation. To implement plans effectively they need to be 'sold' to those who will be involved in carrying them out. This management task requires many other skills: leadership, motivation, delegation, communication and control. But for those organisations able to focus on the benefits of planning, as a framework for dynamic change and growth, success in the rapidly changing marketplaces of the 1990s is much more certain.

Management is about leadership and leaders sell concepts and objectives just as the salesperson sells products. Both are equally essential to the continued health of the business. Internal marketing is a way of selling plans to staff and colleagues so that as the plans become operational there is commitment to their achievement. Internal marketing applies to all managers; it is crucial that every manager secures acceptance and support. Internal marketing is a tool of motivation and support. It builds morale, and provides the rationale for the plans. Otherwise there is the serious danger that plans will be written by 'them' and not accepted by 'us'. 'Them & Us' operations are doomed to misery: high staff turnover, autocratic demands and staff resistance to change are typical results of the failure to market internally.

Internal marketing takes the concepts and techniques of marketing and applies them inside an organisation. This is normally not a big budget operation - but the principles of selling a package hold true. The plan or objective is the package; the employees are the customers. Staff will be more committed to a plan's objectives if they believe in it; if they have 'bought it'. Committed staff who believe in the organisation's plans have a focus, a common purpose. Conflict and misunderstanding are reduced, effort and resources are directed to the achievement of the plan.

Many companies still fail to make plans available to employees and do little to market their strategies - seeing such actions as unproductive. In fairness they also can be concerned with security, but by the time planning has advanced to the level that it can be made public internally there is generally little of which alert competitors are not already aware. One, of course, guards sensitive managerial information extremely carefully.

People are by far the most important resource in any organisation and so activities which improve motivation and increase effective use of the human resource should not be underestimated. Only people have the ability to deliver the competitive edge. Security is a matter of trust, and people can be trusted if well motivated, involved and committed.

TOTAL QUALITY MANAGEMENT

Total Quality Management (TQM): managing the entire organisation so that it excels in all dimensions of products and services that are important to the customer.

Total quality management (TQM) is a philosophy that uniform commitment to quality in all areas of the organisation will promote a culture that meets customers' perceptions of quality. It involves co-ordinating efforts directed at improving customer satisfaction, increasing employee participation and empowerment, forming and strengthening supplier partnerships, and facilitating an organisational culture of continuous quality improvement.

Key dimensions of TQM
- Creative and talented employees empowered with decision-making responsibility and authority.
- Decision-making is parallel and simultaneous. (marketing & production work together - what a concept!)
- Creativity and participation is valued over control.
- Use speed and quality for competitive advantage.

TQM is founded on three basic principles.
- Continuous quality improvement is built around the notion that quality is free and involves building in quality from the very beginning. An important tool is benchmarking, the measuring and evaluating of the quality of an organisation's

goods, services, or processes as compared with the best-performing companies in the industry.
- Empowerment gives frontline employees the authority and responsibility to make marketing decisions without seeking the approval of their supervisors.
- Quality-improvement teams bring together the best and brightest people from a wide variety of perspectives to work on a quality-improvement issue.

Benefits of total quality management include lower operating costs, higher returns on sales and investment, an improved ability to use premium rather than competitive pricing, as well as faster development of innovations, improved access to global markets, higher levels of customer retention, and enhanced reputation. However, few companies are using TQM because it requires a substantial investment of time, effort, money, and patience.

Key problems with TQM
- Not all employees want or should be empowered.
- Employees may not embrace corporate objectives (especially if their own personal and career objectives clash).
- Communication problems can hinder TQM implementation.
- Implementation bureaucracy can bog down an organisation.

ORGANISING MARKETING ACTIVITIES

The role of marketing in an organisation's structure is critical to the success of the plan. Companies using the marketing concept begin with an orientation toward their customers' needs and desires, and they are able to closely co-ordinate the marketing unit with other functional areas. A marketing-oriented organisation concentrates on discovering what buyers want and providing it in such a way that it achieves its objectives. It focuses on customer analysis, competitor analysis, and the integration of the firm's resources to provide customer value and satisfaction, as well as long-term profits.

A true marketing orientation takes a different perspective on a firm's structure. In the traditional hierarchy, top management or the CEO is the pinnacle of authority, and every level of the organisation is under the authority of the levels above it. The marketing-oriented approach inverts this pyramid, placing customers at the top, and every action within the organisation is directed at serving customer needs. Each level must answer to the levels above it, but answering to the next level means taking actions necessary to ensure that each level performs its job well.

Alternatives for organising the marketing unit
Centralisation versus decentralisation:
  a. A centralised organisation is one in which the top-level managers delegate very little authority to lower levels of the organisation.
  b. A decentralised organisation delegates authority as far down the chain of command as possible.

The best approach to organising a marketing unit depends on the number and diversity of the firm's products, the characteristics and needs of the people in the target market, and many other factors. A marketing unit can be organised according to function, products, regions, or types of customers, or a combination.

a. Organising by functions
- Is fairly common because it works well for some businesses with centralised marketing operations
- Can cause serious co-ordination problems in more decentralised firms

b. Organising by products
- Is appropriate for firms that produce and market diverse products
- Gives a firm the flexibility to develop special marketing mixes for different products
- Can be expensive because of the layers of management and employees that it creates

c. Organising by regions
- Is appropriate for large firms that market products nationally or internationally
- Is effective for firms whose customers' characteristics and needs vary greatly from one region to another

d. Organising by types of customers is appropriate for a firm that has several groups of customers whose needs and problems differ significantly.

New trends in corporate management, including **horizontal structures, re-engineering, and the "virtual" corporation**, affect the way marketing management activities are carried out.

1. **Horizontal management structure**
    - Organisational structure built around processes rather than tasks.
    - Levels of supervision are minimised by combining tasks within processes.
    - Teams rather than managers run processes.
    - Performance evaluation based on customer satisfaction.
    - Performance and compensation based on team not individual performance.
    - Employees have maximum contact with supplier & customers.
    - Employees trained for and trusted with critical data and decisions.

2. **Reengineering**: radical redesign of processes for major gains in cost, service, or time.
    - examines the organisation from the outside in
    - designs it around customers' needs.
    - promotes strong leadership from the top.

3. **Virtual corporation**: quickly formed temporary network of joint ventures and alliances to exploit fast-changing opportunities.
    - Conceived as a grouping of independent organisations-manufacturers, service providers, suppliers, customers, and even competitors-that are linked with information technology to share knowledge and skills.
    - There is no central administration, no hierarchy, and no formal lines of authority.

IMPLEMENTING MARKETING ACTIVITIES

A. Motivating marketing personnel
To motivate marketing personnel, managers must discover their physical, psychological, and social needs, and then develop motivational methods that help employees satisfy those needs. Plans to motivate employees must be fair, ethical, and well understood, and rewards must be tied to organisational goals.

A firm can motivate its workers by directly linking pay with performance and by informing workers how their performance affects department and corporate results. Selecting effective motivational tools has become more complex because of greater differences among workers due to race, ethnicity, gender, and age.

B. Communicating within the marketing unit
Good communication helps marketing managers motivate personnel and co-ordinate their efforts. Communication with top-level executives keeps marketing managers aware of the company's overall goals and plans, guides the marketing unit's activities, and indicates how they are to be integrated with those of other departments.

An important type of communication is communication that flows upward from the frontline of the marketing unit to higher-level marketing managers. Marketing managers should establish an information system within the marketing unit to make it easy for marketing managers, sales managers, and sales personnel to communicate with one another.

C. Co-ordinating marketing activities
- Marketing managers must synchronise individuals' actions to achieve marketing objectives and work closely with managers in research and development, production, finance, accounting, and human resources to see that marketing activities mesh with other functions of the firm.
- Marketing managers must co-ordinate the activities of marketing staff within the firm and integrate those activities with the marketing efforts of external organisations.
- Marketing managers can improve co-ordination by using internal marketing activities to make each employee aware of how his or her job relates to others and how his or her actions contribute to the achievement of marketing objectives.

D. Establishing a timetable for implementation
Successful marketing implementation requires that employees know the specific activities for which they are responsible and the timetable for completing each activity.

1. Establishing an implementation timetable requires
2. Identifying the activities to be performed
3. Determining the time required to complete each activity
4. Separating the activities that must be performed in sequence from those that can be performed simultaneously
5. Organising the activities in the proper order
6. Assigning the responsibility for completing each activity to one or more employees, teams, or managers

THE FUNCTION OF MARKETING CONTROL.

Control is the evaluation of marketing performance and outcomes in order to learn whether or not marketing goals have been met, and, if not, why not. Controls provide information that can be used to change marketing plans and their implementation.

Control is extremely important when the competition is intense because good controls can lead to a competitive advantage by improving the efficiency and effectiveness of marketing activities. Control tracks performance and outcomes using such measures as sales, market share, costs, and customer satisfaction.

Many businesses use a marketing audit to determine how effectively marketing is being managed. A marketing audit is like an accounting audit, but only of marketing activities. It is usually performed by an external consultant, someone who can be objective in evaluating how well the organisation is implementing the marketing plan and achieving marketing goals.

THE MARKETING AUDIT is a systematic examination of the marketing group's objectives. Its primary purpose is to identify weaknesses in ongoing marketing operations and plan the necessary improvements to correct these weaknesses. A marketing audit may be specific and focus on one or a few marketing activities, or it may be comprehensive and encompass all of a company's marketing activities.

A specialised type of audit is the customer-service audit, in which specific customer-service activities are analysed and service goals and standards are compared with actual performance. Specialised audits could also be performed for product development, pricing, sales, or advertising and other promotional activities. The scope of any audit depends on the costs involved, the target markets served, the structure of the marketing mix, and environmental conditions.

The marketing audit should:

- Describe current activities and results related to sales, costs, prices, profits, and other performance feedback
- Gather information about customers, competition, and environmental developments that may affect the marketing strategy
- Explore opportunities and alternatives for improving the marketing strategy
- Provide an overall database to be used in evaluating the attainment of organisational goals and marketing objectives

Marketing audits can be performed internally or externally, formally or informally. There is no single set of procedures for all marketing audits, but some guidelines should be adhered to.

- Questionnaires should be developed carefully to ensure that the audit focuses on the right issues.
- Auditors should develop and follow a step-by-step plan to guarantee that the audit is systematic.
- The auditors should strive to talk with a diverse group of people from many parts of the company.

Problems with audits
- They can be expensive and time-consuming.
- Selecting auditors may be difficult because objective, qualified personnel may not be available.
- Audits can be extremely disruptive because employees sometimes fear comprehensive evaluations, especially by outsiders.

CONTROLLING MARKETING ACTIVITIES
The formal marketing control process consists of establishing performance standards, evaluating actual performance by comparing it with established standards, and reducing the differences between desired and actual performance.

A. Establishing performance standards
Planning and controlling are closely linked because plans include statements about what is to be accomplished. A performance standard is an expected level of performance against which actual performance can be compared. Performance standards should be tied to organisational goals.

B. Evaluating actual performance
Marketing managers must know what employees are doing and have information about the activities of external organisations that provide the firm with marketing assistance. Records of actual performance are compared with performance standards to determine whether and how much of a discrepancy exists.

C. Taking corrective action
Marketing managers have several options for reducing a discrepancy between performance standards and actual performance.
- Improve actual performance
- Reduce or totally change the performance standard
- Do both

Improving performance may require better methods of motivating marketing personnel or more effective techniques for co-ordinating marketing efforts. Sometimes performance standards are unrealistic as written, and sometimes changes in the marketing environment make them unrealistic.

Problems in controlling marketing activities
1. The information required to control marketing activities may be unavailable or available only at a high cost.
2. The frequency, intensity, and unpredictability of environmental changes may hamper control.
3. The time lag between marketing activities and their results limits a marketer's ability to measure the effectiveness of specific marketing activities.
4. Because marketing and other business activities overlap, marketing managers cannot determine the precise cost of marketing activities, which makes it difficult to know if the outcome of marketing activities is worth the expense.
5. It is very hard to develop exact performance standards for marketing personnel.

HOW CONTROL RESULTS MAY BE APPLIED IN MARKETING.

Control results may indicate that things are running smoothly and only slight corrections are needed. In other cases, control results may show that there are serious problems, so a more drastic response may be needed. Some U.S. and E.U. companies faced with quality control problems have turned to Japanese quality control methods. This includes *kaizen*, a commitment to continual improvement that seeks to make products and processes better, and thereby enhance quality.

Control results may indicate that changes should be made in product and market mixes or in strategies designed to grow the business.

THE ROLE OF MARKETING IN SOCIETY

Marketing plays a very important role in the life of consumers and society. Some of the ways that marketing contributes is by
- Providing products that consumers need and want
- Offering products at prices that consumers find acceptable
- Placing products where consumers want them, when they are wanted
- Informing consumers about products, prices, and places
- Offering employment to millions of people
- Contributing to the economic health of a nation by encouraging competition and the free market
- Bringing supply and demand into balance
- Helping clear the market of excess supply
- Generally contributing to the high quality of life that most people enjoy

SOCIAL CRITICISMS OF MARKETING

Marketing is criticised for many shortcomings, including contributing to excessive consumption, cluttering society with too many products and promotions, and engaging in questionable practices, some of which are illegal and others are both illegal and unethical.

Criticisms on marketing's impact on society as a whole include marketing creating:
- False wants and too much materialism
- Producing too few social goods.
- Cultural pollution - constant assaults on privacy by advertising and noise clutter.
- Too much political power.

There are six primary criticisms levelled at the marketing function by consumers, consumer advocates, and government agencies.

1. High prices
Many critics say the marketing system causes prices to be higher than need be. Some factors to which these critics point are as follows:
    a. **High costs of distribution.** Greedy middlemen mark-up prices beyond the value of their services. There are too many middlemen and they duplicate services. Retailers have responded by saying that:
- The work performed by the intermediaries is necessary and takes away the responsibility from the retailer or the manufacturer.
- The rising mark-up is really the result of improved services.

- Operating costs are what is driving up prices.
- In reality, retailer profit margins are low because of intense competition.
- Strong retailers pressure their channel members to keep prices low.

b. High advertising and promotion costs.

Marketing is accused of driving up promotion and advertising costs.
Marketers respond by saying that:
- Consumers want more than the merely functional qualities of products, they want psychological benefits.
- Branding gives buyers confidence.
- Heavy advertising is needed to inform millions of potential buyers of the merits of a brand.
- Heavy advertising and promotion may be necessary for a firm to match competitors' efforts.
- Heavy sales promotion is needed because sometimes goods are produced ahead of demand in a mass-production economy.

c. Excessive mark-ups.

Critics charge that some companies mark-up goods excessively.
Marketers respond by saying that:
- Most businesses try to deal fairly with consumers because they want the repeat business.
- Most consumer abuses are unintentional.
- When shady marketers do take advantage of consumers, they should be reported to the authorities.
- Consumers often do not understand the reason for the high mark-up.

2. **Marketers are sometimes accused of deceptive practices that lead consumers to believe that they will get more value than they actually do.**
    a. Deceptive pricing includes such practices as falsely advertising "factory" or "wholesale" prices, or a large reduction from a phoney high list price.
    b. Deceptive promotion includes such practices as overstating the product's features or performance, luring the customer to the store for a bargain that is out of stock, or running rigged contests.
    c. Deceptive packaging includes exaggerating package contents through subtle design, not filling the package to the top, using misleading labelling, or describing size in misleading terms.
    d. Deceptive practices have led to legislation and other consumer protection actions.

3. **High-pressure selling is another criticism of marketing.**
    a. Laws require door-to-door salespeople to announce that they are selling a product.
    b. Also, buyers have a "three-day cooling-off period" in which they can cancel a contract after rethinking it.

4. **Shoddy or unsafe products is another criticism levelled against marketers.**
    a. Complaints are made about products not being made well.
    b. Products deliver little benefit.
    c. Product safety has been a problem for several reasons:
        - Manufacturer indifference.
        - Increased production complexity.

- Poorly trained labour.
- Poor quality control.

5. Planned obsolescence is a strategy of causing products to become obsolete before they actually need replacement and is a criticism levelled by consumers.
   a. Fashion is often cited as an example.
   b. Marketers respond that consumers like lifestyle changes; they get tired of old goods and want a new look.
   c. Much of so-called planned obsolescence is actually the normal interaction of competitive and technological forces in a free society.

6. In contemporary society poor service to disadvantaged consumers is another criticism against marketing.
   a. Better marketing systems must be built in low-income areas.
   b. Action may be taken against merchants who advertise false values, sell old merchandise as new, or charge too much for credit.

THE MODERN MARKETING APPROACH

In *Marketing is everything*, Regis McKenna believes that we are witnessing a marriage between marketing and technology. Knowledge-based marketing and experienced-based marketing are the offspring of this marriage.

This development implies a radically new role for the marketer who will now have to build a sustainable relationship between company and customer. In other words, the marketer of the 1990's functions as an integrator whose task is to synthesise technological capability with (knowledge-based) market needs and to bring "the customer into the company as a participant in the development and adoption of goods and services" (experienced-based). Sustainable relationships with the customer are the key to success.

Some of the consequences of the new developments described by McKenna are given below:
- Marketing is no longer an isolated function but a way of doing business
- Marketing is no longer about image-making in the sense of "creating and projecting a image of the company to lure customers"
- Marketing is part of everybody's job; it is integrated in the organisation
- Marketing is about building relationships with customers.
- Marketing is no longer a bag of tricks
- Marketing aims at creating new markets and not selling products in existing markets
- Marketing is about "customisation", i.e., The capacity to deal with customers in a unique way.
- The new concept of marketing implies the end of the advertising era.
- Marketing implies an ongoing dialogue with the customer
- Marketing entails the "servicisation" of products and "productisation" of services
- Marketing is honesty!